WTF?

(Who's The Fool?)

ISBN-13: 978-1500971250

ISBN-10: 1500971251

WTF? (Who's The Fool?)

CHAPTERS AND TOPICS

CHAPTER ONE: THINGS BEYOND OUR CONTROL – pg. 7

CHAPTER TWO: THINGS RESISTANT TO CHANGE – pg. 31

CHAPTER THREE: THINGS THAT CAN BE CHANGED – pg. 68

INTRODUCTION

Everything we know we learned from our society that is the product of cultural evolution to support the status quo system set up to benefit the primary stake holders, namely the elites. Over time, simplicity is replaced by complexity that hides the truth to keep people in a state of confusion and disconnection from each other, so they will acquiesce and support social order that permits the elites to retain their control over the mechanisms of society that maintains their economic advantages.

This book discusses many of our socially conditioned suppositions that we learned from school, media, parents, and social contacts who exert conformity pressure. Most people go through their lives never questioning who they really are, and why they believe what they believe without question.

CHAPTER ONE: THINGS BEYOND OUR CONTROL

1 - THE BEGINNING
[Where religion and science connect]

God   created everything from an extremely dense ball of ultra-compressed matter about the size of a tennis ball, in the void of space. In an instantaneous explosion all matter was atomized and thrown into the deepest recesses of space, later cooling, to become stars, galaxies, and planets. Time was set into began. This great creation explosion set into motion a unifying set of laws that applied to all future creations and provided continuity to the universe.

The   Milky Way galaxy was one such creation from the expanding matter of the initial explosion, containing our solar system of a lesser star and a dozen planets. Nine planets remained after two collided to create the asteroid belt. The twelfth planet (Planet X), a massive planet of the size of Saturn, was set on an orbit of 200+ million years which takes it 1000 times beyond the orbit of Pluto.

After the earth cooled enough to form an outer crust, on one orbit, Planet X passed near the earth and pulled the oceans and seas into outer space. As Planet X continued at great speed on its 200+ million year orbit, the water that was pulled into outer space froze, and fell back to earth as large masses of ice, which formed glaciers.

As millions of years passed, the ice near the equators eventually melted and once again became oceans, which provided a source of evaporation to create the atmosphere. Large ice formations remain today, covering the north and south poles. At another passing of this great planet, the enormous pull of the planet's gravity deformed the earth's crust, creating mountains and volcanoes from the molten mass inside the hollow earth sphere. Great tectonic plates were set in motion, which continue to shift today.

During one such pass of Planet X, the dinosaurs and most of the life on earth was pulled into outer space (some life on the far corners away from the planet's path, shielded by the earth's mass did remain, but great winds and surf killed most life that was left, except for some creatures in the deepest parts of the oceans that remained). Almost all animal life was sucked into outer space; the cellular tissue which was made from a high percentage of water exploded, with only the bones falling back to earth intact, and the rest falling back as the molecular debris in a chemical and organic stew.

As the land masses that were pulled into outer space fell back to earth, many bones, creatures great and small, and plant life were fossilized as land which was once the ocean floors fell on mountain tops and fields, becoming top soil.

2 - THE BEGINNING OF MANKIND

[Where's the dichotomy between creation and evolution?]

During a passing of Planet X between Mars and earth, it took all the life and moisture from Mars and flung it into the orbit of the earth, and was eventually captured by the earth as it passed through the material in its orbit. The molecular life from Mars intermingled with that on earth, and gave the bio-molecular stew in the earth's ocean and on the continents the additional nutrients and cellular material that evolved into present day life forms, one such evolved into human form (independently of the apes, which evolved separately, but concurrently). Biblical accounts that God created man in his own image, first male, then female from the male, are not inconsistent with evolution.

The process of creation in God's time may be a day; but by mankind's standard, it may encompass millions or even billions of years. Man may have begun to evolved as an asexual being, then during the course of evolution, a mutation occurred, which made the evolving species both male and female, from organic material of the original asexual organism. Subsequently, due to the prolific process of sexual procreation, humans created by sexual intercourse procreated in vastly larger numbers, and asexual reproduction became an extinct human procreation process.

3 - EARTH'S STRUCTURE
[Things are not as solid as a rock]

Conventional theory states that the earth has a solid iron core, surrounded by molten magma, with a thin outer crust. This idea came from observing volcanoes, the magnetic quality of the north pole, and some very limited exploratory drilling and sonic studies.

The fact remains that no one really knows what's deeper than a few miles down from the deepest wells that have been drilled. Not so long ago, scientists and religious leaders believed that the world was flat, and that sailing past the horizon would result in falling off the edge of the known world. It was heresy to claim that the earth was round, and that the earth was not the center of the universe. Would it be scientific and religious heresy today to suggest a more plausible theory about the structure of the earth? Science will eventually prove that the earth is a hollow sphere containing molten magma with a high iron content, without a solid iron core, but with an expansive hole at the north pole that is covered by a thin crust and glacier.

When the universe came into being, as explained by the BIG BANG THEORY, extremely hot expanding matter was hurled into space in all directions. The swirling gases and masses expanded, and as the gases condensed and cooled, became stars, planets, moons, asteroids, comets, and other space matter. The spin of the earth created centrifugal force such that the molten matter vectored away from the center; consequently, the mass expanded outward in all directions toward space. Concurrently, the centripetal force of gravity counteracted the centrifugal force from the earth's rotation, and a spherical shape eventually stabilized.

Since the earth continued to rotate at more than 1,000 miles per hour, the hot, molten matter that was not exposed to the intense cold of outer space remained a moving molten mass, while a cool thin skin formed the earth's outer crust. Weaknesses occurred in the cooling and formation of the earth's outer crust, and internal pressure from the heat and movement of molten magma pressed against the inner surface of the earth's crust, forming cracks in the outer crust and fissures where hot molten matter from inside the hollow sphere gushed out as volcanoes, etc. Eons ago, when the internal heat pressure of the earth sphere became too great, a hole was blown out at the north pole, releasing both gases and magma which were recaptured by the gravity of the earth. This material eventually became part of the earth's atmosphere or fell back as floating continents.

The molten iron alloy subterranean magma rotates in a south to north direction, as it rubs against the inner side of earth's crust. The magnetic field created by the south to north movement of the magma causes compasses to point north. However, the floating outer crust rotates in an almost counterclockwise direction, from west to east. On a near miss by Planet X, the floating outer crust was pulled to a rotation that was separate from the directional movement of the magma.

4 - EARTHQUAKES
[Unpredictable but explainable events]

Earthquakes are caused by various phenomena which interact to create or relieve the stress that is placed on earthquake faults, including:

- increased frictional and gas compression pressure from the molten magma on the inside of the earth which causes the crust to destabilize and crack in the areas of weakness.
- the earth's rotation creates centripetal force which presses the molten magma against the inside face of the earth's crust. This stress against the land mass, (especially at weaken points caused by the uneven cooling of the outer crust which was once molten matter) form various earthquake faults, and provide conduits for surface volcanic activity.
- as new magma is pushed up from the ocean floors through underwater fissures and faults, the ocean bed expands and pushes against oceanic plates which abducts against the continental plates, much of which is land that floats on ancient oceans and molten magma.
- much of the continents was formed by molten magma from inside the earth, which blew out a hole in the north pole as a result of extremely hot temperatures, spewing massive chunks of molten rock which fell back to earth.
- continental drift is caused by the longitudinal movement of molten magma beneath the oceanic plates that expand and push against the continents, which rotate counterclockwise to the east.
- The movement creates pressure against the land masses where the oceanic and continental plates collide, causing cracks in the land mass, and earthquake faults at various depths which are undetectable until after a fault moves and cracks all the way to the surface.

- the location of the San Andreas and other known faults on the "Rim of Fire" in the Pacific Ocean may have been initially caused by a great ancient meteor strike that created the Pacific ocean basin, and may have added to the many faults and instability of the oceanic and continental plates. This meteor strike may have also caused the Biblical torrential rain and flooding for 40 days and 40 nights, when the entire Pacific ocean was blasted into the atmosphere, then eventually rained back down to earth, causing massive flooding until it ran off the continents and back into the empty ocean bed.

5 - ENVIRONMENTAL POLLUTION
[Living in a pig sty]

There exist natural and man-made pollution. Natural pollution includes lightening caused wildfires, excrements from animals such as cows, which appear to have deleterious affects on the upper atmosphere's ozone layer, and droughts which cause massive loss of top soil. Man-made pollution comes from industrial and metropolitan wastes generated by explosive population growth that causes exponential increases in the demand for manufactured products.

It has become conventional knowledge that man-made greenhouse gases is thought to cause global warming, however it is unlikely that is the primary cause when the macro forces of nature underneath the ocean beds and from our sun appears to have created cycles of heating and cooling throughout Earth's geological and meteorological history.

Pollution occurs at every level; at the mineral extraction site; at the manufacturing site; and at the consumption site. Chemicals are utilized in various processes which have toxic affects on living things, such as fish, fowl, plants, mammals, and humans. Manufactured products do not decay back to base elements, as do organic wastes; consequently, both land and water become contaminated with non-biodegradable wastes.

The accumulation of wastes, toxic chemicals, and other pollutants continue to expand in geometric proportions as the onward march for technological progress and financial gains blind people to the fact that the earth is a limited biosphere on the brink of overpopulation and over pollution. The human species has a choice to reduce environmental pollution, adapt to more prevalent pollutants, or eventually to become an endangered, or extinct species. Adapting to an increasingly toxic environment would most likely entail the protection of the elite classes of wealthy powerbrokers, possibly in dome communities, while commoners will continue to suffer in the open unprotected environment.

6 - EVOLUTION
[Survival of the fittest]

Evolution encompasses a theory that species tend to change with time. While the theory appears to explain gradual changes as the result of the natural adaptation of species to their environment over lengthy periods of time, it has not been proven that all species share a common ancestry with the amoeba. It is probable that multiple species were created continuously through natural processes at varying periods, which then evolved, diverged, and multiplied over time in reaction to environmental changes.

Life on earth may have begun away from earth, or have been part of space and interplanetary debris that came with meteors, comets, asteroids, neighboring planets, and from debris caused by the occasional passage of Planet X. There also exist the possibility of deliberate genetic introduction or manipulation by superior beings from other more advanced extraterrestrial civilizations. Consequently, evolution may be comprised of natural, supernatural, and extraterrestrial forces working independently, but interacting together to effect genetic changes in terrene species.

Natural selection states that species which are better acclimated to the changing environment tend to survive in greater numbers than those that are less suited to the environment; consequently, over a lengthy period of time, if placed in competition for survival, the "superior" species is that which best adapts to its environment, while the least adaptive species will become extinct.

If we study mass population statistics, in most developed nations, the female of the human species outnumber males, outliving men by several years due to many reasons, both hereditary and environmental. Extrapolating even a 1/10th of one percent annual increase in the longevity of women as compared to men, over another 10,000 years, there will be 10 times more women than men. Science and technology, coupled with changing societal norms, will soon foster in the day when women may procreate without male participation to eventually create a superior race of women. In the distant future, the male may become an endangered species, to be replaced by women.

Population statistics also indicate that better educated and higher income individuals live longer and generally more disease free than people from lower economic classes. Manmade selection will augment natural selection as this law of nature will become secondary to institutionalized rules promoting survival of the wealthiest. Here again, women are making great strides through inheriting wealth from their husbands, and extrapolations indicate that increasing wealth and longevity will ensure a future female survival rate that will be superior to that of men.

But long before that time, the entire human species may become an endangered species, subject to extinction due to catastrophic upheavals in the earth's ecosystem that may be created by any singular or interaction of various destruction scenarios (e.g., collisions with massive renegade comets, asteroids or meteors, massive earthquakes and volcanic activity, incurable diseases, nuclear war, destruction of oxygen by pollution of oceans and destruction of all rain forests.

7 - EXTRATERRESTRIAL LIFE
[We are not alone]

Probability dictates that with millions of galaxies in the known universe, containing billions of stars, and most likely trillions

16

of planets, some of which support life, many of which may support intelligent life; it is likely that in the 15+ billion years lifespan of our universe, that many civilizations have developed, then expired over the eons, and that many superior civilizations may exist, compared to our human civilizations of only 5,000 years.

The ETs have been observed, painted, written about, spoken of, and now filmed and videotaped by hundreds of thousands of people during mankind's existence. The unreported accounts probably far outnumber the reported accounts with observers generally having been considered normal and sane. It is highly improbable that conspiracies of UFOlogists or crazy people could account for the thousands of mass UFO sightings during the course of human history.

Men once believed the earth was the center of the universe, and thought the world to be flat. This self-centeredness remains the main obstacle to the realization and acceptance, that based upon probable causes, mathematics, empirical data, and even religious references in the holiest of books; that intelligent life exist in ample quantities in other parts of the universe. If only our science were capable of propelling us to distant galaxies, or to peer into the deepest recesses of space to prove the premise that humans do not occupy the highest level of intelligence and civilization in the known and unknown universe.

8 - NATURAL DISASTERS
[Endless complexities and cycles]

Massive natural environmental changes have occurred throughout the eons, long before the advent of humans. These changes continue today, and will undoubtedly continue after mankind is no longer a viable species on planet earth. As with all natural phenomena, earth is in a constant state of flux.

Changing weather patterns, oceanic temperatures, atmospheric composition, wind strength and direction, continental drift, seabed accretion, fault stress, tidal patterns, flooding, drought, volcanic eruptions, and topsoil erosion and depletion are the norm, and not the exception.

Human beings have been largely successful in adapting to the changing face of the earth, and to a lesser degree has been the architect of environmental change due to construction of cities where forests once flourished, creating lakes by damming rivers, and other superficial projects. Yet, humans are infants when it comes to affecting natural phenomenon, and are ill equipped to stop natural disasters. No building has ever been built that can not be toppled by a super earthquake. Few homes exist that can survive a Level 5 tornado or hurricane head-on. With the exception of large dams, no structures exist that can hold back torrential rain and flooding. And no defensive system has ever been built that can shoot a meteor, asteroid, or comet out of the heavens before it hits the earth. Humans are fragile surface dwellers in a constantly changing hostile world.

9 - OVERPOPULATION
[Choking on too much of a good thing]

How many people can mother earth support? As the population has exploded from 1 billion to almost 6 billion in less than one century, it is projected at the present rate, the planet will be drowning in 50 billion people within the next century. But long before that time, there will be pandemic deaths from incurable diseases; mass starvation from crop failures caused by hostile weather; great wars between many nations fighting over land, religion, or greed; reduced life span due to poverty and environmental pollution; and massive lost of life from natural and nuclear catastrophes.

In nature, only those species that can adapt to changes in the environment continue to survive. Human beings are still bound by that fact. In nature, when the numbers of certain species become too large to be fed and supported by the natural environment, famine, disease, and starvation kills a great number, thereby trimming the herds and flocks to that which can co-exist in the limited environment. When the human population exceeds the limits of the environment to nourish such life, massive famine, disease, and starvation will trim the herds and flocks in the cities and megalopolises. Perhaps governments will fall, anarchy will reign for a time, then a new cycle of order will be restored as the reduced population becomes manageable again.

10 - PROPHESIES
[Untapped brainwaves]

There have been throughout recorded human history the existence of prophets, whose visions of the future have become realized as historic facts; where their teachings have brought a sense of peace and acceptance to a disorderly world during times when people endured great physical suffering; and when fear of the unknown was laid to rest by visualizing a better future. When events unfold as foretold by prophets, it is unclear if the power of suggestion effectuated the events, or if in fact prophets can have knowledge of events that have yet to occur. Perhaps prophesy is no more than the ability to recognize the relationship of natural laws, as in foretelling that a person will fall into a pit if he doesn't walk around it.

Abraham, Jesus Christ, Buddha, Mohammed, and other spiritual leaders have founded systems of beliefs that provide the behavioral foundations for the vast majority of humans. Morals, ethics, and family values are commonalities throughout the world's greatest and most popular religions. Perhaps the prophets were sent to us from God, the first Creator from the beginning of time. Perhaps lesser gods from other worlds sent these prophets. Or perhaps these were men who became anointed in their divine tasks through the use of their mental capacity to connect with the endless universal thoughts that hitch rides on carrier waves and photon beams.

Einstein once postulated that we utilize no more than 5% of our brain's capacity. Could it be that some sections of our human brain houses processes such as mind-reading, prophesy, astro-projection, and pyschokinesis, in addition to memory, reasoning, visualization, artistic talent, motor control, and intelligence? Experiments, though not completely conclusive, appear to suggest that in some rare cases, a high probability of reliable can be established in some people's ability to demonstrate extrasensory perceptions and paranormal skills.

11 - REINCARNATION
[Living once is plenty]

No one can prove with empirical evidence the existence of past lives. No one can prove with empirical evidence that the existence of future lives do not exist after physical death. No one really knows. In dreams, many people claim to have memories that don't conform to their known lives; and under hypnosis, they possess demonstrable abilities, personalities, skills and talents that they have never learned nor possessed in their conscious lives. Fantasies, deception, or reality? Is it possible that some memories can be inherited via DNA, thus enabling progeny to recall episodes that they have not lived in their own current lives? Does this qualify as reincarnation? Does part of our soul, our life force, become imparted to the seeds of our propagation; thus are we in part reincarnated?

Does it matter one way or another? We can only live in the present, as singular physical beings. Many people choose to live in the past or future, by claiming reincarnation, time travel, alien abduction, or whatever. These imaginations may appear to be real to the perceiver, and may possibly be real in fact; however, it is not demonstrable to others who can verify its existence; consequently, since it can't be proven, it doesn't change the physical reality that we live in. When a tornado flings a house a mile, perceivers believe it because the evidence is clear. When a person claims to be another who has lived in the past, the evidence is not clear.

12 - RELIGION
[The opiate of the people]

Human's have had a historical, perhaps even genetic propensity toward explaining the apparently unexplainable through various religious thoughts and beliefs. Religion gave hope to the downtrodden and to those who suffered in the face of great and persistent adversity. Religion allows people to accept their realities, because it permits them to feel that either it is all right to suffer, or that a better life exist after death, thus suffering should be accepted and dignified in the present. The ruling classes almost always had the favor of the organized religious leaders and cleric, who condoned their royal decrees and power to exploit or oppress the poor. Common people were taught that they were born to suffer at the hands of authority, to acquiesce to it, and to pay tribute to it. Meanwhile, people of authority did not feel the need to experience the suffering of the masses.

What if the majority of people were to believe that it is not reasonable to suffer or to pay taxes and homage to rulers; that happiness and good times, and physical pleasures were their inalienable right of pursuit; and that rulers and governors should have to feed and clothe themselves? What if most people were to believe that there is no afterlife, but that they had only one shot at life here on earth? Certainly we would see the demise of organized religion, and an insistence that equality should exist between the ruling class and their subjects. But changing the status quo, as we've seen, requires complete upheavals to the political and bureaucratic infrastructure of societies. It is not likely that many groups of people could organize grassroots movements that can overthrow the status quo.

13 - SPACE TRAVEL
[How can babies fly before they can crawl?]

Humans have barely been in space for 40 years, with space exploration limited primarily to our own back yard, our solar system. The present forms of vehicle propulsion greatly limit the speed at which space craft may be propelled, thus lengthening the time required for space travel. People from the ranks of science who believe in UFOs and in extraterrestrial flying saucers are open to discovering new methods of propulsion. Two such systems may be possible.

First the nuclear method would be similar to that of firing a bullet from a shell casing. We could build a 1,000 feet deep cylinder well; a 4 feet diameter tube, lined with a 10 feet thickness of Teflon at the bottom, tapered to one feet thickness at the exhaust port on the surface, two feet thickness of titanium steel alloy throughout, and encased in four feet thickness of lead casing throughout. At the bottom of the well would sit a conical chamber that is 100% iron or granite that is at least 100 feet thick. At the end of the well that attaches to the top of the enclosed cone shaped chamber, would sit a projectile shaped instrumentation vehicle that is 4 feet wide (with one feet thick walls constructed of titanium/carbide steel). The projectile's base would be constructed of 200 feet of solid high temperature steel alloy and would sit even with the base of the well where it connects to the top of the conical chamber.

A measured nuclear discharge would be set off, inside the conical chamber, thus providing the vehicle with propulsion up the well cylinder, and out into space. Increasing nuclear yield would increase the speed of the vehicle, and if it were possible to transfer a maximum portion of the energy dispersion from the nuclear blast to the vehicle, then speed could approach the speed of light. This method could probably be limited to non-manned vehicles, as the G-forces would surely crush any living organism.

The second method requires controlling the emissions of sub-atomic particles. First a field of high density hydrogen atoms must be created, such as H16 (probably using an atomic accelerator). These hydrogen atoms would be highly valence negative, seeking electrons to balance their atomic configuration. An external electron gun would shoot out a controlled beam of free electrons from control jets. The entire vehicle that is engulfed in high density hydrogen would propel itself in the direction of the electron beam, and since the beam would be traveling at the speed of light, the spacecraft's speed could be controlled by varying the density and frequency of the electron beam bursts.

That is why flying saucers are capable of great speeds and turning in directions that seem to defy gravity. Where the electron beam is pointed is where the vehicle will travel; unlike vectors as is normal for fuel propulsion travel. In addition, UFOs do occasionally vent excess hydrogen gas, thus the glow and color changes that are normally associated with UFO sightings. The effect of the high density hydrogen would attract free electrons, such as that from power lines and car batteries, causing the common observation of loss of power during close UFO flybys.

14 - TECHNOLOGY
[Simple attempts to solve complex problems, or
complex attempts to solve simple problems?]

Technology, like most human advances, continue to change people's daily lives in very pervasive ways. However, technology is not the panacea for all human problems, and in fact, often act to create new problems, such as massive underemployment.

In many instances, depending upon the tasks to be performed, a live interactive human being is more efficient or cost-effective than robots, machines, computers, and various technologies. All machines need to be serviced, otherwise they break down with wear and tear. They are not completely tireless. They overheat, blow fuses, short out, grind out gears and bearing, need oil changes, and parts need to be replaced. That means downtime and inefficiency.

It is not possible for present day machines to be maintained and serviced without human beings. High-tech demands high investment of capital. Even with relatively minor changes that humans can immediately adapt to, computer software would need to be rewritten, machines would need to be reset, and in many cases completely redesigned and re-machined by humans.

Corporations are discovering that it is often less expensive and more efficient to employ people to do the work that was once earmarked for high tech robots and computers. It would take a far stretch of the imagination to visualize a world where machines would do everything for humans. If for no other reason, people need people, as we are social animals most of the time. For most parts, humans are still the most efficient machine ever created, operating for hours for the price of a few hamburgers. But, technology is here to stay as sure as the change from riding horses to driving automobiles.

In spite of limitations that are peculiar to either machines and/or people, some exciting technological discoveries are on the horizon that can be of great benefit to humanity. Humans are within a decade of producing automotive engines that run on electrolysis of water, diseases that can be cured by micro focused irradiation with picowaves (that kill viruses including AIDS), flying via positronic emissions and electromagnetic repulsion, deep space travel via high intensity controlled negatronic and magnetic flux bursts, supersonic flying cars, thought-projection amplification, skin and hair regeneration via stem cells, non-organic food substitutes, and encapsulated nutritional concentrates for enhancing physical, emotional, mental, or sexual performance.

A humanistic life supplemented by technological progress which solves the problems of human societies, rather than adding to the destruction of the earth, would be a noble and necessary goal for technology. We don't need another weapon system that is capable of destroying all life on our planet, with the exception of planetary defense against rogue comets or invasion by advanced ETs.

15 - TIME TRAVEL
[If you believe it's concentric, parallel loops]

Einstein's Theory of Relativity suggests that since it is impossible to travel faster than the speed of light, then time travel would not be possible. He suggested that if it were possible to travel near the speed of light, that matter and time would compress, making it unlikely that humans could exist under such conditions.

How do we know for a fact that travel at speeds greater than light is not possible? Has anyone tried lately? Didn't humans once believed that speed greater than sound was not possible? And travel to the moon was only the fantasy of science fiction writers and movie makers. Let's take the limits off our hypothetical parameters and postulate what would happen if we could observe from earth events happening 15 billion light years away, almost instantaneously. Light that was emitted 15 billion ago from the time of the BIG BANG now reaches our part of the known universe. The light that leaves the earth will take over 5 billion years to reach the edge of the expanding universe that is comprised of younger galaxies.

If we had a way to observe events that are happening in the present time, anywhere in the universe, would this entail the necessity of time travel? Or would the phenomena be similar to changing the stations on a television set...instantaneous. When our telescopes pick up light and radio wave emissions from distant parts of the universe, it represents events of a distant past. Light from a center point that reaches 3 places in 3 different galaxies that are equal distance apart from each other, as in a isometric triangle, would all witness events from a similar time period of the past in each place.

Each of the 3 places would witness the same events from the center point; however, all would witness a different past in respect to the others. How then is it possible to travel into the future, or into the past? Time travel? Let's hypothesize that science is able to solve the physical problems of traveling faster than the speed of light, such that we could be anywhere in space, in the twinkle of an eye. Would that be considered traveling in time? In respect to events as they would occur, we would witness them in the present; however, we would be able to go to distant places, with announcement of impending events, and would appear to have knowledge of future events as viewed by distant places. Yet, we could not physically travel into the future to experience events that have not yet occurred, nor go back to events that have already happened, to change events, to create a different time line and history.

Time appears to be linear in the physical world, and while speculation exists of parallel universes due to the vastness of space and the existence of anti-matter and other anomalies that do not conform to our 3 dimensional world, there is no evidence that we in our current physical states would be able to maintain our existence in environments not conducive to our life form's survival. Perhaps it would be possible to have mental experiences by tapping into other dimensions; however, no physical proof has ever existed of dimensional or time travelers, as the physical form as we know it prohibits it.

16 - WAR AND DEATH
[The final outcome]

War appears to be a method of natural selection and population control to counter-balance the prolific tendency of human beings to overpopulate the earth, thus becoming an ecological threat to the ecosphere, the balance of nature. It would appear that war is a manmade phenomena, but studies of animal societies and insect communities indicate that overpopulation leads to massive aggression and warfare.

Humans may be playing out the process of natural selection, but people think they are in control of the process. If humans are in control of this aspect of natural selection, then why can't we turn wars on and off at will? Why does it almost always entail great casualties, before human societies resolve their differences, when the stronger conquers the weaker through massive wars of destruction or attrition? The worldwide scale wars like the Napoleonic, WWI, WWII, Hundred Years War, Roman and Trojan Wars, and the Crusades had a real effect of trimming back the population of their time. Were we to experience WWIII, a nuclear holocaust will place the human species on the brink of extinction. Those who might survive would produce a mutant progeny, thus new species would occur as result of natural selection, survival of the fittest.

Most humans who subscribe to religious thought believe that death is only the end of our physical existence, that our souls continue, remaining alive in spirit form, until such time as it is given eternal life or destroyed by God at the end of time as we know it. At the end of physical time, the temporal nature of our existence ceases to affect our souls, as the soul's immortality renders linear time inapplicable. Or, perhaps there is no life after death, and our perception of reality, presence, or even dreaming ceases upon physical death. Perhaps there is only life or death; existence, or non-existence. We can only surmise, as not one soul has come back to prove the existence of a previous or future lives.

CHAPTER TWO: THINGS RESISTANT TO CHANGE

17 - AMERICANOMIC SYSTEM
[Same game by a different name]

America is being raped by the corporate greed of the international pirates that include the leadership of the largest multi-national American, Canadian, European, and Japanese corporate conglomerates. American executives now earn an average of 100 times the wages of the average worker, even during times of mass lay-offs, large corporate losses, and bankruptcies. The European and Japanese executives earn 10 to 50 times the wages of their average workers, and they are still successful. The global community is regressing to a stage of feuding nation-states, where the economic disparity that exist between the ruling classes and the masses once again becomes legitimized by its institutions. The wealthy minority dominates the majority poor, and the primary purpose of the consumer classes is to provide a vehicle of profit for wealthy equity holders.

Despite so-called experts who perpetually disagree with each other, the economy can be explained in rather simple terms and concepts.   There are four basic components of any economy; first, natural resources; second, manmade goods and services; third, distribution; and finally, value that is created by demand.   When any of these economic elements become unbalanced, the economy skews toward those who controls any of its elements. When any particular group controls the first three components, they develop a virtual monopoly on the fourth.

Different political systems utilize laws to alter the natural relationship between these four elements of economy to shift wealth from its unprotected classes (the poor and consumer classes) to its protected classes (the economic and political powerful).

If left alone, without governmental restrictions, except that transactions should be based on a doctrine of mutually fair exchange of similar value (of whatever equivalent method of trade), economic systems would naturally tend to become balanced systems. Name one person who would knowingly consent to a barter situation where his own interests becomes secondary to making a profit for the other guy. With the legitimizing and collusion of special interest government, the economic interests of the average citizen is subrogated by the self-perpetuating interests of the power brokers who attend to the economic interests of the ruling class, depending on special interest support to maintain power.

Institutionalized inequities are more apparent in certain industries than in others; however it pervades the entire economic structure of America, is legitimized by government, and is taught in universities as the way things should be, further perpetuating a system that primarily serves the will of the wealthy.

18 - THE AMERICAN PIPE DREAM
[Why 99.9% will never become wealthy]

The vast majority of people are not born with a silver spoon in their mouths, and did not inherent great fortunes. A few will on the strength of desire, determination, hard work, and luck, will manage to cut out a nice slice of the American pie. Most people, however, will barely eke out a living, month-to-month, and will retire on the hope that the Social Security minimal subsistence system will not go bankrupt as they wait in line.

Those who take up the challenge of attempting to become wealthy discover a multitude of external obstacles to attaining fortunes. First, they usually begin with insufficient capital or financing. In order to obtain funds, they must turn to various potential sources of financing, which means giving up control over the idea or business in order to obtain investment capital. First timers face an inability to raise capital without assets or credit to serve as collateral or to bolster their creditworthiness.

On the other hand, the established wealthy individuals have alternate sources such as letters of credit, signature loans, etc., and even after defaulting on large amounts, and can still raise additional funds. Donald Trump is one such example, being on the brink of bankruptcy, he was allowed to restructure his debt through borrowing more money! Let's see the average tax-paying hard working, law abiding citizen get that kind of a break!

Many people sometimes find inspiration to come up with a good idea. The next step is to obtain patent protection, right? Again, it's not a simple and inexpensive task, as the invention laws have been written to benefit large corporations by giving the wealthy people through their lawyers the right to challenge, stall, and steal ideas from inventors by use of the courts. Another prohibitive strategy is the high cost to obtain and maintain patents, usually exceeding $10,000 for a simple claim. Large corporations and the wealthy have legal and research departments and consultants at their disposal; but the struggling individual has only his determination, courage, hard work, dreams, and what little life savings he can muster to go up against a system that discourages inventions from individuals.

It is high time that the patent laws should be changed to encourage and not discourage new ideas from brilliant individuals who do not fit into the corporate machinery. Added protection must be obtained in foreign markets to prevent cheap imitations from flooding U.S. and world markets, without compensation to the original inventors. The prohibition against marketing prior to patent issuance is simply another method to support the status quo from having to compete with new products that would cut into the profitability of their existing products, or cause them to pay for costly retooling for new products.

Should the small inventor survive the expensive and time consuming process of obtaining a U.S. Patent, the risky process of taking the invention to production, then to market almost always incurs even greater prohibitive expenses. The cost of mail order averages about $2 per name (factoring in mailing list, printing, postage, envelopes, and labor), which promises only an average 3-5% response rate, and maybe a 1-2% sales ratio. Newspaper, magazine, radio and television ad rates are also substantial. Informercials on cable television are still relatively excellent buys, but the cost of a professional ad spot can be significant. The adage, "it takes money to make money" certainly rings true.

Once the individual inventor succeeds in fighting off all apparently insurmountable odds, he faces the likely challenge, exploitation, and theft of his invention when duplicated from confidentially disclosed patent information which then becomes public knowledge. Corporation lawyers and imitators are well posed to keep their challenges in the courts until the small inventor goes broke from legal fees, or dies from decades of frustration and worry. The net effect is that small inventors do all the work, as the parasitic forces of wealth wait in the shadows to usurp the profits that are rightfully due the inventor.

Well, if you can't beat them, then why not license the invention to a corporation? That works, if it means that your competitor would save more in attorney fees than what royalties they may have to pay. Read the typical corporate non-disclosure agreement, and it is full of loop holes, whereby they can walk away with the inventor's ideas without paying one cent of compensation. They always claim that it was an idea they were already working on, or that it is the same as other products already on the market, or that it is not a new idea, and so on. Corporate greed compels them to resist giving the real inventor even one percent or one cent.

Most people will not venture to dive into this process because there exists ample internal obstacles to attaining their financial goals. Fears and inadequacies, lack of appropriate abilities or skills, lack of an emotional support network (to offset negative pressure, doubts, criticism, and ridicule from one's spouse, family, and so-called friends), lack of determination and persistence, lack of funds or financial backing, lack of motivational rebounding ability, lack of resources and investment network, lack of self-belief and self-confidence, lack of vision and courage, and lack of willpower and self-motivated drive soon sabotages individual spirit to fight on.

19 - BANKING AND CREDIT
[Is anything safe?]

The explosive growth in the number of failed and failing banks, savings and loans, and other lending institutions is endemic of a failing system based upon an abrogation of basic good economic sense. Banks were initially places to deposit savings and valuables as an added measure of safety and security from outlaw forces. The evolution of banking created corporate entities whose purpose was no longer the protection of depositors' assets, but the reinvestment of those assets for the purpose of making a profit for the investors.

Consequently, corporate greed and governmental acquiescence and collaborative guarantees permitted the banking interests to invest in very risky ventures such as loans to third world governments and foreign companies, dry oil wells, real estate scams, and unproven technologies; all with substantive losses that were "written off" the books, meaning the taxpayers footed the bill for billions of dollars in bad loans made by American lending institutions.

Average Americans couldn't get a loan for a business start-up during the same time wheelers and dealers were using letters of credit and loans to raid solvent companies, leaving them straddled in excessive long-term debts. And now, many of those takeovers have resulted in the bankruptcy of the shell of what were once successful American corporations. Of course the corporate raiders have long since run off with their $ billions in profits that have directly resulted in the loss of hundreds of thousands of jobs. These greedy corporate raiders should not have been admired, but rather they should have been jailed, just as the head of the failed Lincoln Savings and Loan was jailed for preying on and destroying the lives of untold thousands of people.

Historically, the seeds of the failure of the banking system lies in the special interest influence of banking industry executives on governmental regulators and politicians whose laxities have resulted in a system that is out-of-control, insolvent, and has violated the trust of its depositors.

Government makes an ineffectual regulator when its lawmakers and officials implement fiscally irresponsible laws and regulations that have encouraged lending institutions to make highly risky investments that should not have been permitted at all. Now, again the taxpayers are stuck with the enormous expense of bailing out insolvent institutions.

Solutions to the banking problem as another weakened leg of the American economy must first start with an examination of the concept of "credit." Creditworthiness is the cornerstone of lending. An individuals ability to qualify for a loan is normally evaluated against his credit history, and the future prognosis of timely repayment of a loan. The interest rate that is charged to individuals for the use of the lender's money is tied to the level of risk that the lender takes in consideration of a borrower's assets, income, existing debts, reputation, employment and credit history.

Somehow, basic lending principles applied to working-class individuals are often disregarded when large loans are made to corporate executives, corporate raiders, large corporations, and foreign governments and entities. We are now learning the lesson that apparent "bigness" does not insure solvency. Every time a large corporation goes belly-up, untold thousands of workers and related businesses are hurt, and the taxpayers absorb the bill for bad loans made by lenders to large corporations because lending criteria and practices that are usually applied to evaluating individuals are disregarded when dealing with the economic elitist class.

The cost of credit is another area that has become essentially unregulated. It was once usurious and illegal for individuals to charge more than 10% interest on a loan (to deter loan sharking); however, we now find that the biggest loan sharks are institutional lenders, auto financing companies, thrifts, and the government itself. Credit cards at 21% interest, car loans carried by dealers at 24% interest, appliance purchases carried by thrifts at 21% interest; and late payment interests of 25% per year plus 25% penalty for uncollected taxes (that adds up to 50%), and parking ticket fines that are doubled if not paid in full by the stated bail date (100% penalty). Any excessive interest payments decreases the net productivity of individuals. If a man earns $2000, but pays $500 for interest payments, $500 in taxes, and $700 for rent and utilities, that leaves him very little for food, transportation, clothing, and "living". He is essentially broke. He would otherwise be solvent if his debt payment were only half as much.

The biggest scam in credit is the idea of compound interest. If you loan the bank $1000 (when you open a savings account, you are actually lending the bank your money) at 10% interest, you will have $1100 after one year. If you do not touch your money, at the end of two years, you will have earned 10% of $1100, or $110, for an aggregate total of principal and interest of $1210. When the bank lends your money out, they need to recover the amount of interest that is paid to you, plus an amount for profit. If the bank loans your $1000 out at 15% per year for two years, and schedules level term repayments, the borrower repays 30% interest or $300. The bank makes a $90 profit ($300 income from borrower minus $210 paid to depositor) which translates to 43% on the amount paid to the depositor. Actually, the borrower never has the entire $1000 to use, because he starts repayment after one month. And that amount of money that is repaid by the borrower is loaned out again. That's why deferred payments on auto loans increases the vehicle price by 50% over a 4-5 year period, and the actual price of a home is paid 3 times over a 30 year period (with the first 20 years of payments scheduled primarily to interest payments).

The solution should be the elimination of compound interest, and a reversion to simple interest. If one borrows $1000 at 15% per year, the bank should be paid interest only payments of $150 per year for each year that the $1000 is outstanding, with the principal to be due at the end of the term of the loan. This enables the borrower to actually have the full $1000 available for his use during the term of the loan. In addition, the burden of monthly repayment would become manageable. The borrower would be required to purchase affordable government guaranteed loan insurance, and deposit a reasonable percentage of the loan principle into a government escrow account (this could be the FDIC insurance escrow account). In the event of default, the insurance company and the governmental escrow account makes the bank whole, including interest. The defaulting borrower is assessed a reasonable percentage of the defaulted loan balance still due after security instruments are sold off to satisfy partial repayment of the original loan. Any balance due is divided into payments according to a sliding income schedule, and collected along with withholding income taxes until the deficiency judgment is satisfied.

The U.S. Treasury is a political mechanism that is too much under the control of a few. Allowing one man to set interest rates is too much power to give to anyone, and in the future could foster a greater unequal distribution and waste of government dollars by supporting welfare for the rich through manipulation of the value of money and interest rates to benefit specific sectors of our economy, primarily the wealthy who receive various tax breaks and incentives and subsidies.

20 - ECONOMICS SIMPLIFIED
[Or a confusing shell game]

The basic concept of supply and demand appear simple enough. For example, if ten people lived on an island, and the only source of food was fish, and there existed 10,000 fish, it's likely that the value of each fish would be such that fish could be used in barter to obtain other goods and services. However, if there were 10 people and only 100 fish, the value of each fish would increase such that people would desire to barter other goods and services to obtain fish. If there exist a limited supply of anything of value, its value will increase as a result of any increase in the number of persons having a demand. Taking the same example, if only 100 fish existed, but an abundance of fruit trees grew in the wild, then the value of fish would decrease because a demand for fish would decrease due to another food source.

What happens to confound the natural relationship between supply and demand is the effects of mass advertising. Sophisticated marketing techniques coupled with the vast influential power of high tech telecommunications has the effect of magic... the use of smoke and mirrors and slight of hand to fool the average consumer into making decisions based on deception and impulse. Creating desire (demand) based on slick techniques to convince the American consumer that particular products are more valuable than they may be in reality. Thousands of companies have bought into the concept that advertising on television and other mass media improves their market share. The tremendous cost of mass advertising is always passed on to the consumer in terms of higher product prices.

Advertisers like to call this "value added", when in fact it is usually nothing more than waste and deceptive packaging on a grand scale to mislead the general public into buying products that are worth less than the price that they are charged. We would all be paying $500 for stainless steel toilet seats if the average American was as stupid as the government buyers. Fortunately, most Americans still possess some common sense.

Value is a fluctuation of human desire, an emotion that can be manipulated by cultural and societal influences. Scarcity of products desired by people will cause the value of those products to increase; however, scarcity for undesired products will not increase the value of unwanted products. Mass marketing is a method by which psychological suggestions are made within the context of societal and cultural dispositions to effect an emotional response pro or con pertaining to a particular product, service, or idea.

Value is a subjective emotional perception that does not require factual content. Stocks and bonds, insurance, and other forms of speculative investments are primarily based on a perception of future value. Something with no intrinsic value can be marketed to create a demand. Fads come and go, just as people's desires peak and wane; consequently, value is sometimes an illusory and fleeting phenomenon. However, without value, trade and economy could not exist. Without value, no wealth, and no methods to amass fortunes would exist to die for.

21 - INSURANCE
[Your fears, their profit]

Insurance was a clever notion that was initially developed for the common good. The concept of insurance was the pooling of money by many to contribute to a common savings to be utilized in the event of disasters that may be suffered by its members. Like other once noble ideas, insurance has evolved into another form of legalized gambling (not unlike the stock market). Here again, the public is persuaded to hand over up-front money on a potential promise of future benefit.

The public bets that ill-fated events will inevitably occur, and insurance companies wager that that death and mayhem will strike only an insignificant proportion of the population at any particular time. And they have scientific data, actuary tables, and other sophisticated methods to prove that they are right. But the fears of the American public has made the insurance industry one of the most formidable special interest group in America, after the oil industry, agribusiness, and banks.

Californians passed a law to require rebates on excessive overcharges by insurance companies, yet legal maneuvering, delays and defiance has demonstrated the true power of the industry, permitting them to prey on the deep rooted fears of the public to make excessive profits while to defying the will of the people.

Ask any widow, accident, fire, or burglary victim who has received an insurance settlement, and they will swear by the goodness of the industry. Ask anyone who pays exorbitant insurance premiums, who has never received (and most likely will never receive) an insurance settlement, and they'll swear they're being ripped off. Both groups are correct. Individuals do need assistance during times of great personal loss. Insurance is a viable method, where the collective assets of a large group can be brought to bear on the losses of a significant few. The problem does not lie in the basic premise. It lies in the implementation of the concept.

"Whole life" is sold as a savings plan, where policy owners may even borrow against their own investment, and pay the insurance companies additional interest payments for the use of one's own money. If one survives the term of the policy, the entire amount invested is returned as a retirement income, plus a small sum of interest. As a savings or retirement plan, anyone would do better to buy U.S. Savings Bonds.

When purchasing only the "protection" component of insurance in the form of "term life", the savings portion of a whole life policy may be invested in the bank at an average higher return than is offered by most insurance companies. Rates charged to insure a particular auto or home varies wildly, and depending upon the insurers, rates that target various sectors of the consumer market may differ in excess of 300 percent. Consequently, consumers need to become informed shoppers.

Consumer confusion in understanding insurance policies and the insurance industry speaks well for exploring a joint public-private insurance arrangement. The government should offer insurance guarantees, not unlike that offered for real estate loan programs such as FHA, Fanny Mae, and Freddie Mac. Government would guarantee premium payments during such times that the policy holder is out of work, and unable to meet his monthly payments. This would be especially helpful in the case of providing health insurance coverage to all Americans. All insurance companies would routinely deposit a certain percentage of the collected premiums into an insurance guarantee fund, that the government would use to pay insurance companies for lost premiums until individuals could find employment and are reinsured by their employers. Employers whose size makes it infeasible to provide health insurance coverage would also deposit a specific amount into the insurance fund based upon their number of employees, and the government would contract out to approved insurance carriers or public hospitals for major medical coverage that is competitive and affordable.

22 - THE MIDDLE CLASS

[A promise of diminishing returns]

A redistribution of wealth from the rich to the poor, socialism, returning to a basic barter system, or any revolutionary change in the economy is not suggested. Positive changes should develop in prudent, predictable, and incremental steps to minimize the systemic shock that invariably results in great suffering for the vast majority of people. We should not dismantle all the positive institutions and systems that exist, but instead improve and encourage the development of a more motivated, productive, and wealthy middle class to ensure a diverse economic foundation that can survive in the global economic markets. We need not repeat the mistakes of either the People's Republic of China or Russia.

Strengthening the middle class creates consistent markets for more products and services while providing the wealthy class greater opportunities to amass even greater fortunes. The larger tax base enables government to provide needed infrastructure improvements, funds to reduce the federal debt, support of social programs, national defense, and technological advancement expenditures. The shrinking middle-class can have a devastating effect on the economic survival of our nation, and decreases opportunities for both domestic and international businesses. While many cash fluid rich can increase net worth a hundred folds during a recession or depression by their ability to buy property at highly discounted prices from those who are cash starved, the long-term devastation of a recession or depression actually decreases the amassing of fortunes when compared to economic boom periods.

The real causes of economic recession are the imbalances that are created when vast sums of money leaves the country from an imbalance of trade, the exporting of American jobs by both American and internationally-owned companies, and the uncontrolled runaway debt incurred at all levels of the economy, from individual to corporations and government. Presently, the total net worth of all the property in America has been estimated at $50-55 trillion.

The gross productivity of the economy (GNP) is approximately $4.5 trillion per year, and the federal budget about one-fourth of the GNP. Federal, state, and local taxes and user fees now account for about 40% of the average household's expenses. The top 1% of the population owns one-third of all the wealth in America (the top 5% owns almost two-thirds), the bottom fourth owns less than 5% of America, and the middle-class owns the balance (30%). America is rapidly becoming a two-class society, of the rich versus the poor.

Mankind's history is filled with examples of civilizations whose governments were eventually toppled by the poor after the disparity between rich and poor become obscene and inhumane.

23 - THE STATUS QUO
[What's really going on?]

The effects of almost 50 years of economic, political, and social evolution has resulted in a fragmented nation, floundering in the tides of time, without purpose and direction, lacking in resolve and self-confidence. Europe and Asia have prospered greatly since World War II; however, it now appears that America is positioned for a long slide, and many Americans may have to accept a standard of living that is equivalent to that of developing nations.

Most Americans still believe in the great ideals of freedom, democracy, and self-determination; however, a problem lies in the confusion over the definition of constitutional concepts, resulting in more conflict and disunity among the citizens. Many Americans no longer know what it means to be "American." Is being American simply worshipping the sanctity of a common flag? Is being patriotic the code word for being anti-foreign, especially anti-ethnic? Ask 100 people on the streets, and probably no more than a handful can list the first ten Amendments to the U.S. Constitution, known as the Bill of Rights. Many people would mistaken it for a socialist manifesto.

So who should we blame? The Japanese for the unbalanced trade? Certainly their unfair trade practices have engendered a resurgence of anti-Asian racist attitudes among the American rank and file. But if all things were equal, and each American bought $1 of Japanese goods, and sold them $1 of American goods, there would still be a trade deficit because there are twice the number of American consumers as Japanese. The Japanese would have to amass a total disposable income twice that of Americans before they could buy $2 of American goods for each dollar of Japanese goods sold to America.

Should America kick out all the foreigners, and keep America for Americans only? That means repurchasing over $1 trillion in European ownership of America, and over $250 billion in Japanese ownership of America, which is about all the money our federal government collects in taxes each year. And as we attempt to turn back time, why not make international air traffic illegal, and make all international trade agreements null and void?

Let's nationalize all foreign-owned businesses on American soil, and boot out these aliens. We have enough natural resources to sustain our population indefinitely, and we could aim all of our nuclear missiles at every nation in the world who may be a threat to our xenophobia. We could develop a great patriotism and national pride based on a "us against the world" fantasy.

The frightening part of this scenario is that millions of Americans would vote for such a platform today, just as sure as the 55% of white voters who once favored electing a professed racist during the election for Governor of Louisiana (but Mr. Duke lost due to the non-white vote). During times of economic downturn, people look to extreme and fundamentally un-American notions to deal with their problems. As long as our political and corporate leaders continue to satisfy their own needs before the interests of America, then this extremist scenario may be inevitable, and the seeds of a second civil war may indeed be sowed. Then the militias may turn out their new battle cry for a separatist nation.

Fortunately, may rational Americans are still in control. This is a nation of explorers and malcontents who fight to the end. How we can each help to affect positive changes in our individual lives and make the changes needed in the self-perpetuating institutions that have fostered a system of mediocrity and failure in America for the past generation? How can average Americans save America?

If the American experiment fails, then perhaps the future of mankind will rekindle the homogenous warring nation-states era of history. And in an age that is already proliferated with nuclear weapons, it would not take but a few zealots and terrorists to touch off the beginning of the end.

It has become even more essential to the survival of mankind that America must recover its confidence and resolve. America must prove that the strength of American ideals enables people from all countries, races, ethnicities, cultures, religions, and gender to share in a fair and lasting prosperity. If America sheds its commitment to individual freedom and progress, then the world is doomed to more warfare that may lead to human extinction.

24 - THE STOCKMARKET MENAGERIE

[Outta sight rumors]

A baffling contradiction appears in our economy today, where the stock market posts record highs, breaking the mythical 5000 barrier while unemployment remains high in many sectors of the economy. If we count everyone who is on welfare, homeless, underemployed, or who have given up looking for work, the unemployment numbers would double!

Why, at a time of great stockholder profits, are companies going bankrupt and thousands are losing their jobs? Where is all the money going? Why are the profits not being reinvested into companies to maintain jobs? Are the wealthy class, armed with inside boardroom information, taking advantage of institutional investors such as pension plans? When counties lose billions of dollars in the stock market game, who is winning those dollars?

Taken as a group, investment experts are no more effective in predicting the future value of stock than flipping a coin or throwing darts blindfolded. Studies have shown that chimpanzees make better stockbrokers than most of the pros. The real money is being made by those with the inside track, friends of corporate management who are leaked insider information, and can make clever buy and sell decisions that is subsequently mimicked by the public sector institutional investors and John Q. Public. The lag in time between insider trading and the movement of large blocks of public sector stock equals big profits for those clever private investors who are able to buy low and sell high. It's a simple case of the horse leading the cart. Of, course, our government regulators are blind to it.

When companies first go public, and make a stock offering, investors buy shares of stock to provide needed capital for company growth, on the potential promise of future performance. Depending on the eventual growth of the company, the number of times the stock is split, and the amount of stock that is retained by the company, future stock value may have little impact on providing significant additional capital to companies for additional growth. Shareholders become the beneficiaries of stock profits, and the process of stock trading moves real and paper profits among the various investment portfolios of investors, but may have little beneficial effect on providing needed reinvestment income to companies.

The improved value of a company's stock translates into increased creditworthiness, and permits companies to "borrow" capital on the open market, and decreased stock value severely limits a company's ability to borrow money. The irony is that companies that borrow get deeper into debt, and this has a potentially negative long-term impact on the stock value of the company.

We see it all too often. Stock prices go up, investors take their profit out for the short-term kill, without regards for the long-term solvency of the company. Large long-term institutional investors, and the public are left holding the bag. So when the value of the stock market goes up, the slower moving institutional investors and the less informed average investor will benefit along with the stock manipulators (however at a lesser proportionate gain per share); however, when things start to sour, the horse drops the cart and heads for greener pastures, while the cart remains stuck in a gully, and takes the big losses.

The stock market is a macrocosm of an investment club. With investment clubs, individuals pool their capital to support the economic well-being of their investment choices. The basic premise is sound, and provides a means of more rapid economic growth to companies. The hope is that the increased operating capital provided by investors will translate into a company growth rate that significantly exceeds the amount invested, thereby providing a handsome dividend to investors, even after a company assumes additional debt from borrowing outside of the investment group.

Without the invention of investor clubs that evolved into the stock market, and the legal creation of the perpetual corporate entity, the great economic boom of this century could not have been possible. But are times changing? Is all of this paper profit actually beneficial to the economic strength of American industry, and therefore the nation as a whole? Or is the system set up to benefit the sophisticated mobile class of wealthy investors who move money internationally among the major stock markets, sometimes to the disadvantage of American corporations?

Why should our national confidence be based on the health of the stock market? When the market is up, the rich become wealthier, yet the ranks of the poor increases as middle-class Americans find themselves in unemployment lines. This happens because money not paid to employees is reallocated to pay for larger executive salaries and bonuses, and to increase the return on investment to shareholders. When the market is down, employees are laid off to provide savings that again translates to protecting the investors and corporate executives. Either way, the working-class gets shorted. A double blow comes when the market is down, and workers' retirement pension programs that are invested in stocks lose value; and consequently lessens or wipes out their retirement protection.

The solutions are simple. The short-term and especially the long-term health of corporate America, and consequently American jobs, would benefit from the stability that would be created if investors were required to reinvest a significant amount of capital back into the companies to support the infrastructure of the company (improvements in plant, equipment, and workforce) and to reduce the net effect of debt.

For instance, if at the time an investor sells his shares, the stock value has increased by 20%, then 20% of that increase should revert to the company's reinvestment fund, leaving the investor a net gain of 16% over the purchase price. This may encourage investors to invest for the long-haul, adding to the stability of American corporations.

Obviously, something must be done to curb the outrageous incoherent compensation plans given to corporate executives without regard to corporate performance. Executives, who are responsible to manage America's industries in a responsible way, should have a particularly high stake in reinvesting a significant portion of their profits back into their corporations. Exercising stock options to take out $ millions from a company, receiving 100 times the salary of the average worker, abusing the company expense accounts, and setting themselves out as a special class of power brokers who wine and dine with politicians, showing little respect to their rank and file workers, and professing other megalomaniac attitudes have only weakened America's economy.

Would a good father keep 100 times the average family income for himself, while the rest of the family lives on a near-starvation diet? This is exactly what corporate executives are doing to its own family. And with each American family whose breadwinner is laid off and cast into hardship and self-doubt, having to depend on public assistance programs for survival, America suffers as a nation. And when the welfare pots politically vanishes, these disenfranchised Americans will undoubtedly turn to crime, including blowing up buildings.

25 - TAXES AND THE FEDERAL DEBT (1995)
[Toss out the bath water!]

The federal government has now incurred over $1 trillion in national debt, and pays 25% of its taxes collected annually toward interest payment on that debt, operating on a $250 annual deficit. This amount will grow to over 30% by the year 2000, if not sooner. America has borrowed heavily against its future income, on the expectation of greater future productivity, erroneously based on an aging and retiring population, a decreasing number in the workforce, and decreased industrial output and annual Gross National Product. It certainly sounds like a page out of bankruptcy court.

The possible solutions are basic and must be applied simultaneously. First, more income is needed to offset the increasing debt payments. Secondly, expenses must be controlled, wasteful spending eliminated, and greater value for the dollar must be sought for each dollar spent. Third, new borrowing must be severely curtailed, loan repayments restructured over a longer term, and new borrowing to pay existing debts must be avoided. Finally, the dollar must be gradually devalued against other international currencies against an acceptable level of inflation. This will also act to inflate the prices of imported goods, and decrease the relative costs of our exports; consequently, improving our balance of trade, creating more American jobs, and resulting in a higher tax basis that translates to more income for the government to offset the federal debt.

Proposed capital gains tax breaks for the rich must be accompanied by a domestic reinvestment criteria to deter pulling out of profits from local businesses, and further requiring reinvestment of the tax savings into the American economy. Any program of tax breaks designed primarily for the rich with no strings attached will only add to the exportation of American jobs to cheaper overseas labor forces, or adding to investment in non-job producing investments such as antiques, rare coins, and paintings. To move boldly into the future, we must encourage investors to invest in the mechanisms of the future, such as factories and product research, and discourage tax breaks for investing in non-productive commodities such as gold futures, and other non-employment producing articles.

26 - WEALTH
[The game of kings and emperors]

Economics is taught in elite universities, yet all of these experts (who perpetually disagree with each other) have been unable to predict the actions of the economy with any measurable degree of accuracy. Much of the development of economic theories served to bolster the careers of so-called expert academicians, many of whom can not even balance their own checkbooks. Proposed complex economic models and theories, such as Keynesian economics, supply-side economics, Reaganomics, and other approaches, when implemented have created serious imbalances in the economy that usually benefited the wealthy classes.

When we eliminate the technical sounding jargon of theoretical economics, and apply common sense (as in dollars and cents), economic relationships can be explained in simple terms and concepts based on the law of cause and effect. There are four basic components of any economy; first, natural resources; second, manmade goods and services; third, distribution; and finally, value that is created by demand. The collective manipulations of the powerbrokers who control portions of these economic elements causes imbalances, and result in economy conditions that skews toward those who controls any of its elements. When any particular group controls the first three components, they develop a virtual monopoly on the fourth.

Different political systems utilize laws to alter the natural relationship between these four elements of economy to shift wealth from its unprotected classes (the poor and consumer classes) to its protected classes (the economic and political powerful).

For many centuries, nations with formidable merchant and military shipping had the power to control global economic forces. In the recent past, the railroad, oil, automobile, and banking industries have exercised awesome control over the forces of the economy. Railroads gave way to air and trucking; oil became undermined by Arab excesses; the auto industry declined in the face of strong foreign competition; and unsound banking practices eroded depositor trust.

The strength of most of these power industries of the past were primarily based on controlling the means of distribution. The new era of information processing has permitted technologically driven industries to make fortunes. Telecommunication, electronic media, and computer hardware/software advances permitted a quantum leap in information processing efficiency. Technology had its greatest impact in two areas; first in improving manufacturing quality and efficiency, and second in cybernetics, by providing almost instantaneous feedback on the effects of decision-making. Information technology provided business with the means for better internal control and simultaneously created new direct marketing opportunities through telephone and television.

Information technology has produced new powerbrokers who will have an increasingly pervasive effect on influencing almost every aspect of our lives, and will gain a place among the traditional groups that have controlled the economy. Yet, even without information technology, life can go on. It is not essential for bringing the basic necessities to doorsteps of the middleclass consumers. Food and shelter must still involve the human element, the pickers, builders, and drivers. While computers now assist in designing homes, and in ringing up prices at the supermarkets, people are still needed to build houses and to bring the food to the stores... at least for the foreseeable future.

The human element (though to a lesser degree) is still required to keep the wheels of the economy going. Information technology by itself does not permit control of the economy, but assists those groups already exercising significant control to increase their ability to control economic factors.

The oil industry still exerts the greatest influence on the economy; however, health care, pharmaceuticals, information technology, telecommunications, and insurance are making great strides in affecting economic factors. Corporations that control significant portions of these industries will further increase their share of the economy, enabling them to dictate prices without regards for the natural effect of supply and demand.

Back during the late 1960s and early 1970s, a major national labor union was almost able to position itself to greatly influence the price of food, except for the opposition of the fledgling United Farm Workers Union. Any group that is able to control a natural resource, labor, and distribution would be able to control prices, and consequently demand for that product.

Agricultural mechanization has reduced much of the labor intensiveness of food production; however, had that union national union succeeded to organize farm workers back in 1965, they would have controlled the labor of food production and transportation, two of the 3 economic elements needed to control supply and demand. And if representation of the supermarket checkers could have been wrestled from the AFL-CIO, then the chain of food production from the fields to the dining room table would have been complete.

Presently, the greatest threat to low food prices is the growing elimination of small farmers, resulting in a concentration of control of natural resources in the hands of giant agribusiness conglomerates. Artificially manipulated food shortages are not too far off in the future. Of course the excuse for unconscionable food price increases will coincide with a period of drought.

27 - WORKER SUFFRAGE
[Let them eat cake]

The typical American worker has lately been characterized as being lazy and illiterate. Americans work a shorter average work week than the Japanese. So what? Before collective bargaining, corporate abuse of the American worker was severe. Twelve to sixteen hour days and six day work weeks were common. Child labor was a disgrace. Working conditions were hazardous and contemptible. Workers finally exerted their collective voice for humane treatment, resulting in the rise of unions and protective legislation.

Much of America's economy growth occurred during a period of unionization. With the gradual demise of union influence during a period characterized by more responsible employee protection regulations (due in part to unions taking on the similar insensitive attitudes as traditional management, corruption, and lackluster gains for its employees), we have seen a corresponding decrease in worker productivity.

When unions were active, workers felt a sense of banning together for common goals, to demand fairness from management. The sense of camaraderie created a pride that translated to a reputation for hard work and quality products. Widespread employee rights legislation took the thunder out of the union movement. Why should workers pay high union dues to obtain the same benefits and wage increases that would be provided by employers without bargaining units?

After President Reagan fired all of the air traffic controllers who were on a union strike (and banned them from future federal employment), the public realized how ineffectual unions could be. Unionized workers who stuck the Los Angeles Herald-Examiner newspaper never received a raise, nor got their jobs back. Instead, the paper eventually went out of business. These absolute attitudes of non-compromise and disregard for unionized worker rights by government and big business send a strong message to the American worker... if you strike, take a hike.

The American worker was steadily becoming demoralized. Job security was no longer a viable concept. It would not be uncommon for workers to experience unpredictable and periodic lay-offs when various sectors of the economy would experience recessions as the indirect result of political, corporate, and international manipulations. Technology has rapidly changed the face of the American work place, realigning the biological clock to the pace of computerized mechanisms of work, from the office to the assembly line.

The workplace is becoming a dehumanizing experience. It became unlawful to express personal opinions, and the exercise of the freedom of speech often resulted in punitive sanctions by the employer or governmental agencies. Workers not only had to worry about job security as a function of economic factors, but had to be concerned about the idle things they said at the workplace that might be interpreted by people as being sexist, racist, or anti-gay, etc. Interpersonal relations had to suffer as a people became reticent to expose their true feelings.

While restraint may have had a superficial effect of smoothing the superficial relations at work, a deep undercurrent of estrangement, alienation, and demoralization of the American worker has developed, often leading to greater long-term stress-related problems, even to cause violence. Worker dissatisfaction statistically translates to increased absenteeism caused by on-the-job injuries, illnesses, and personal leaves; consequently, decreasing worker productivity. To make matters worse, executive compensation is often at the expense of worker layoffs. Let the workers eat cake.

An attitude of let the workers be damned, and blame the workers for America's economic woes is fostered by many who attempted to focus attention away from the real causes of America's economic problems... corporate greed, decreased reinvestment in the means of production, overextended credit debts, exportation of American jobs, control of economic factors by a minority of the wealthy elite, and politicians who feel more responsible to special interests than to their electorate.

The American worker built this great nation. When the American worker is healthy, the nation's economy is healthy. When the American worker can not earn enough to be the mass consumers of the products of industry, then the economy will suffer. If corporations can not sell their goods, then they too will suffer. Each dollar earned by a typical worker is recycled in the internal economy 7 to 10 times, creating additional jobs and economic opportunities. American's have a rich tradition of being resourceful, and the vast majority of new jobs since 1970 have been created by small businesses during the same period when corporations have been laying off millions of workers to increase corporate profits and executive compensation. The wealthy powerbrokers are sowing the seeds for worker rebellion.

Corporate executives must realize that in the long run, the prosperity of their companies are directly proportional to the prosperity of their workers. The American worker can become a formidable foe to corporate interests when pressed to the wall.

Corporate America has been able to obtain pro-business special interest tax breaks and legislation only because the average voter had been relatively satisfied, and disinterested in political action. A dissatisfied electorate can be a formidable foe to politicians who they believe have lead to their economic misfortunes; and consequently, could elect a new breed of responsible politicians who would be more responsible to worker interests. Only short-sighted corporate executives would fail to recognize that keeping the American worker happy is good for business and long-term corporate health.

28 - WORKING THINGS OUT
[If only special interests would step aside]

While the principles of solutions are basic and simple, the actual solutions to our problems are complicated by conflicting interests of people who stand to gain or lose whenever changes occur to upset the status quo, and consequently pose a potential threat to their economic power base.

Solutions abound. Many things can be better utilized; water can be a better source of energy; the value of gold, gems, and precious metals can become less speculative, and more realistic. An accurate assessment of supply and demand, utilizing data that is readily available to the general population is another method to provide economic predictability and security (so long as the data is easily verifiable and difficult to manipulate). Perhaps the time has come for a more reserved attitude toward evaluating performance, profit and loss ratios. How much is acceptable speculation; why do we take big changes to market products with little or no real value, just for the sake of wealth building?

Most world governments are in collusion with the international class of rich and powerful people. They send their nation's young men to die in wars to protect their national interest in Middle Eastern oil, and structure laws to benefit the rich while the commoners are going to bankruptcy. New ideas are suppressed or stolen in order for the status quo to get the most out of existing products; consequently, it usually takes 5-10 years for most new products to penetrate consumer markets, unless pushed by large corporate concerns. Sure, there are occasional success stories.

There are some sure fire solutions to America's problems, only if enough average Americans would jump on the bandwagon. We need to take steps to safeguard inventors from having large corporations steal their patents by keeping them in court for their natural lives, or until the small inventor goes broke. Other obstacles to progress include our dependency on oil and automobiles, defense industry big ticket items, and corporate greed. We need to improve the economy of all Americans, the poor, the middle-class, as well as the wealthy. We can not rely on our superpower role in improving world conditions until we first get our own house together. So often, history has shown that American intervention in the internal politics of foreign nations has usually made things worse because it creates additional chaos and upsets the basic infrastructure and relationships inside other countries.

Overpopulation in the developing world is a serious problem that threatens the viability of the human species on planet earth. It is a natural flow of evolutionary balance for mass deaths from various causes, including disease, insurrection, and starvation. Humanitarian aid to the world's hungry should be led by private charities who wish to express their religious conscience, and then only supplemented by government in the event of crisis. Too often, foreign aid to other nations only encourages and supports those who already weld political and economic power, with little going to assist the disheartened and downtrodden. Our attempts to solve all of the world's problems only compounds the long term effects on the environment, and by supporting one military or political faction over another, creates new enemies.

Education has always been pronounced as a foundational solution to all of society's ills. We now see a surplus of college grads taking menial jobs to survive. In the future, increase computing power will make our environment user friend, and will require little education to operate. In fact, schools, teaching, and learning will be subjected to new forms and competitive rules, becoming more personalized as computers become all pervasive.

The power of television will be manifested in the new at-home schooling options, nurturing a new type of student who will redefine success, rightness, and will eliminate notions such as failure from our vocabulary. Education will become voluntary and not mandated by statute, as different classes of children become motivated to satisfy their own need for intellectual and social growth. Computer animation, virtual realty, and interactive television shows will create new avenues for recreation and sports.

Are technological advances solutions, placebos, or the poison to the social fabric of our future society? What do people do when their jobs are replaced by technology? Even jobs at McDonalds Hamburgers will be phased out someday. Computerizing world data to improve distribution of resources to areas of need, avoidance of overbuilding to maintain an ecological balance, and improving information accessibility could help to balance the rough spots that feed the causes of poverty, crime, and violence.

Solutions must be found to constructively deal with the poor who are rapidly becoming the majority in America. What part of the problems are rooted in governmental actions, and how can private concerns be further encouraged to provide viable solutions? How can we have progress within a context of environmentally sound industrial growth, while assisting in the course of world development, which would create new markets for American goods?

The social system will undergo profound changes due to changes in the workplace, government, communities, churches, attitudes about conformity, environmental pollution, AIDs and illness, world government, parenting, child abuse, childcare, family stress, grandparenting, divorce, healthcare, gender and race relations, greed, and entertainment.

The political system will resist change, but there will be much pressure to institute computerized voting from home, and people will push for the replacement of politicians who owe their jobs to special interests lobbyists. Telephone, television, computer interactive voting will enable direct democratic participation in a real democracy. This will be possible due to instantaneous data analysis simultaneously across all time zones. We have too many laws, and a push will be made to eliminate old and useless laws for every new law put on the books. Eventually, technocrats will replace politicians, with a mandate to serve people's needs.

The governmental bureaucracy will shrink greatly as people will be able to take care of governmental matters directly from their computers, telephones, or televisions. Bureaucratic penalties will decrease as government redefines its mission. Instead of being the self propagating status quo machine, public servants will act as advocates for the people rights and interests. Government will no longer exempt itself and corporate industries from laws that are exercised on common citizens. The purpose of laws will stress justice and fairness, and not punishment and fines as ways to feed the criminal justice system.

Government will no longer suppress small businesses to keep corporations in control of the economy. The role of the police and courts will be to stay out of the business of law-abiding citizens, and to concentrate instead on the capturing and conviction of violent criminals and other societal predators. The funds for government will not come from income taxes, but from user taxes, so people may have a voice in how much government they really want through the frequency which it purchases public services. The ideals of democracy and freedom, fairness, equality in the eyes of God and men, justice, and free trade capitalism has attracted people from all over the world to emulate this great nation. It's time for America to set a shining example for the world to see.

CHAPTER THREE: THINGS THAT CAN BE CHANGE

29 - AMERICANISM
[It's not apple pie, or a melting pot... it's stew]

Most Americans spring from a common historical heritage; seekers of a better life, greater freedoms, and escape from their motherlands. With the exception of black slaves who were kidnapped from their own native lands, the original settlers of what became the United States of America were a dissatisfied lot. They came to a new land for many reasons, including escaping criminal prosecution, escape from social ostracism, to gain greater individualism, and to gain opportunities that were rumored to abound. But these early European explorers and settlers also brought with them propensities for aggressiveness and violence, rebelliousness, restlessness, violence, and other characteristics that enabled them to conquer the native American peoples, to take a nation away from its inhabitants without guilt due to "Manifest Destiny."

The type of European people who came to America during the earlier half of the 1900s also shared the desire to escape the bad times of their nations, and to start a new life free of problems from their past. The influx of Asian, Latin, and Middle-Eastern peoples that typified immigration in the later half of the 1900s added cultural and religious beliefs that were unusual and vastly different from European cultures.

With the increased immigration of peoples from foreign ands, America is no longer a melting pot, where the minority became assimilated and "melted" into the majority culture. Instead, America as it nears the beginning of another millennium, is more analogous to a stew, where a variation of distinct flavors and stock is jumbled and stirred together. Whether the recipe will be a palatable dish is constantly being judged before the world. Whether the flavor will satisfy its citizens is still out to the jury.   The new problems that always come along with change demand new creative and effective solutions that recognizes the significant differences between a melting pot and a stew.

30 - BEAUTY
[In the eyes of the beholder, until age dims the vision]

Pushed by the media's pervasive influence to set trends and styles, that create great monetary profit, the focus on beauty has focused on the development of external physical attributes and pretentious personalities. People by the millions have become consumers of many techniques to improve their public image through cosmetics, diets, exercise, surgery, dozens of proven and hundreds of untested methods. While vanity make-overs appear to satisfy people's need to feel good about themselves, a lack of emphasis on internal character building is clearly evident. Are so-called externally unattractive persons who focus to develop internal attributes such as compassion, consideration, sensitivity, understanding, and love any less beautiful that glamorous models?

69

Is a single mother who works two jobs to raise her children, with little time or resources to invest in her external appearance, any less beautiful than popular famous actresses? And what happens to people who have had physical attributes as they age and see themselves lose their external beauty? Where is their feeling of self worth, if they had neglected to build character on the inside of their skin? When people become elderly, they find that the basis for true beauty is a deeper sense of self since the external appearances fade, and old folks physically become as equals again, as when they were born.

31 - BENEFIT
[Just give us the bennies]

Under all guises and rationale, whether motivated by charity or by selfishness, people take actions that are designed to bring benefits to themselves. They enter into relationships, business agreements, and affiliations try to manipulate various social situations that may provide emotional, mental, physical, or financial benefits that are self-serving. What rational person gives away their treasures for no reason, or just because its there? There would be endless lines to their front door.

32 - BOOK SMART
[It's what you do with it]

People whose sole or primary source of knowledge is from reading books usually lack the experience and the ability to make realistic decisions and assessment of situations that are not previously covered in their syllabus. Knowledge in itself is a collection of unrelated data, without order or form. The ability to analyze, integrate, and apply knowledge to one's daily life to provide appropriate information for beneficial decision-making is a form of intelligence.

While books provide various blueprints to guide a person in the real world, it is rare for a person's reality to be completely identical to that found in the world of books. Consequently, book smarts in itself fall short of being the most effective vehicle for navigating the potentially turbulent waters of life. Book knowledge, combined with action based on deliberation provides a foundation for appropriate and meaningful experiences, thereby decreasing the frequency of random mistakes that are the usual outcomes of actions based entirely on trial and error.

33 - COURAGE
[Acting in spite of fear]

People who show remarkable bravery and courage in the face of death are driven to overcome the feeling of fear. Courage is not the lack of fear, but the emotional strength to set it aside against real danger, and to take unselfish action to deal with an immediate life threatening situation. Sometimes, immediate heroic response to danger may result in the loss of one's life, the price of bravery.

Reaction to circumstances that are apparently beyond one's ability to control often require that people give everything they have, including their lives. The courageous actions of individuals inspires others to look at their own selfishness and cowardice, and to question how a person could stand up against overpowering odds, even for a moment. Without courage, there would be less justice and truth in this world. People who have the moral conviction to speak and act without regards to the onslaught of imminent danger remind others of the high value of life and the frailty of existence. We are all humbled in the shadows of great men, whose courage set them apart from the flock.

34 - CREATIVITY
[A brain is such a great thing to waste]

Human beings are superior to other animals through our inherent ability to create. People are far more creative than they give themselves credit for; unfortunately, most people do not focus their creativity to complete their projects. People let good ideas flash before their eyes, just to evaporate into the air. Most do not make an effort to write down their ideas and insights on a consistent basis. Many people have become millionaires from one idea. Amazingly, people have million dollar ideas regularly, but fail to recognize it, or to act on it. There are many sources of creativity: dreams with tales from the subconscious; free-association ideas from the conscious mind; inventive and innovative concepts from the semi-conscious mind; and poetry inspired by strong emotional or mental inspiration. By utilizing more focused thoughts,

I have imagined and recorded the plots for almost 100 books, software, games, and movie scripts. I regularly use the process of recording my dreams and visions upon waking. Over 380 inventions and innovations came to me while reading books and magazines, watching television programs, or performing activities. Poetry flowed to me while listening to emotionally charged music or during times I had been excited about a new love interest or relationship.

Most people have regular creative thoughts that they fail to write down. People regularly waste their precious brains when they don't make an effort to tap into the creative force that flourishes inside each persons' mind. There is no reason why people can't have good ideas that can benefit humanity thereby enriching the lives of all. The only required tools are a pen an a blank writing tablet. There are few acceptable excuses for failing to record the gems of that regularly materialize in the human mind.

Ideas are like dollars in the mind bank. Without adding them up, a person doesn't know how much is stored and available for withdrawal or use, or if the funds are being lost. A good idea vanishes if it isn't grasped from the thought stream by recording it. People often rack their brains, trying to retrieve ideas or fleeting thoughts that were great ideas, but were lost because they failed to write it down. That's money out the window, or an insight that could produce more happiness, gone. And maybe gone forever.

35 - CRIME & PUNISHMENT
[Individual crimes and institutional guilt]

People who commit crimes often do not consider their behavior to be criminal. Shouldn't a crime always be a crime? Instead, some acts that are not crimes are legislated into crimes, and some things that should be crimes, instead are not considered crimes. Punishment often does not befit the crime. Why do some murderers go free after serving less than 10 years in prison and some marijuana smokers get sentenced to life in prison depending on their state of residence?

Why is the firing squad or the guillotine considered cruel and unusual punishment, yet it is sudden and painless? Prisons are cages where the weak are preyed upon by the cruel. Why is it not consider cruel and unusual? A man goes to prison for drunkenness, can become sodomized, assaulted and emotionally destroyed by other inmates who are imprisoned for rape, armed robberies, assault, murder, and other violent crimes. These criminals prey on the weak. Isn't it cruel to put at the convenience of harden violent criminals people who, except for a few social mistakes, would otherwise be good citizens?

Is it fair that a person incarcerated for drunk driving should be beaten or gang raped by other inmates because his race is different, then perhaps even to catch AIDS, thus in effect the government dispenses a death sentence for the original victimless crime. The criminal justice system needs to separate victims of social and medical disorders like alcohol and drug abuse, from property crimes, and especially from violent crimes. These three prison populations should be segregated, and not allowed to intermingle; otherwise more career criminals are bred, as proven.

Which crime is greater?   Unfair punishment is a crime against people.   A "de facto" death sentence for drunkards, and freedom for murderers. When certain crimes are "victimless", except for the offender, why do we not rehabilitate them with medical treatment to restore their sense of self-worth and value to their communities?   Instead, we debilitate them by incarcerating them with career criminals, who behind prison walls are the final arbiters and chancellors of what amounts to crime universities, turning out on parole hardened anti-social graduates.

If a certain crime is committed in one place, why is the punishment greatly different than were it to be committed somewhere else, and in fact may not be considered a crime at all in another jurisdiction? Is that equal justice, or just the wrong venue? Unless justice becomes universal, and is not dependent on where persons may find themselves at any particular time, there can be no real justice.

36 - DISEASE & HEALTHCARE
[Till death do you part]

When we have money and health insurance, the doctors and hospitals want to keep us alive, even in vegetative states, when death would be a kinder option. However, if one is poor or penniless, one does not receive the same level of care, even if one desires to live. And when insurance companies or HMOs decides in favor of corporate profits over the value and sanctity of human life, and denies necessary treatment to prolong life, then who are the institutionalized murderers?

When a person helps a critically ill person to voluntarily end their own lives as a humane option to intense and long-term suffering, that assistant is considered a criminal, a murderer. But, when healthcare insurers, management organizations, and providers withhold humane and necessary diagnosis and treatment to avoid corporate expenses, and people die as a direct result of this intentionally cruel negligence, why aren't these corporate gold diggers brought before the courts as accomplices to murder? Patients who want to live are forced to die because corporate profiteering is legal and in the capitalistic spirit. Terminal patients who want to die, aren't allowed to die with dignity because it is illegal. Something obviously doesn't make sense here.

37 - ECONOMIC CONTROL
[The hands that feeds who?]

The rich have always exploited the labor of the poor to increase their wealth from the times of kingdoms to present time. The accumulation of wealth gives the rich the ability to gain power through purchase of intellectual services, physical labor, loyalty of persons on the payroll, political influence through granting of financial or pleasure benefits (bribes, kick-backs, trips, gifts, women, etc.), and the access and manipulation of vast amounts of data through technology. Traditionally, the ruling classes have had both the backing of the military and clergy, controlled the media, economic, and educational systems. Common people have been manipulated through cultural, educational, and religious beliefs and rituals to conform to the status quo. And those who do not conform are subjected to economic sanctions, ostracism, rejection, ridicule, and imprison-ment. The ruling classes through their network of agents control the economic infrastructure, passing rules, regulations, and laws which insure their prosperity, often at the expense of the disenfranchised and disinterested taxpaying citizens. The faceless masses who provide the labor and markets to support the economy of a society are lulled or intimidated into sheepish behavior, rounded up by the sheep dogs, and led to market for slaughter, for the profit of the shepherd.

38 - EDUCATION
[Let there be light, so all may see]

Slave owners always wanted to keep their slaves ignorant because the lack of knowledge prohibited slaves from awareness, functionality, and the development of an ability for the mass communication of their intellectual and political sentiments in the quest for justice and an economic base that wasn't dependent upon the slave owner's resources. While slavery has been politically outlawed in the world for about one hundred years, a form of economic slavery has been perpetuated through inferior educational opportunities that are provided in poor areas that affects all ethnic groups, but primarily colored peoples.

Education or gaining useful knowledge has been, is, and will continue to be the great equalizer and emancipator especially during this highly technological age that is dependent upon instantaneous computer-aided communications that has pervaded the economic system.

The difference between a formidable and applicable education and an inferior education both reflects and translates into real economic disparity between the rich and poor, reinforcing an economic cast that dooms the poor into a lower class from the day of their birth. While highly motivated individuals of the lower socio-economic classes may eventually surpass many deficiencies in their educational environment through the personal pursuit of higher educational goals, the vast majority will succumb to the educational and environmental deficits so prevalent in their communities.

Properly applied, computer and video assisted instruction could become an educational equalizer between the economic classes; however it is likely that the rich will have the benefits of superior software and instructional programming that requires superior equipment hardware. Unfortunately, after two generations of students, we find that antiquated teaching methods are still largely utilized, while video and computer media is rarely utilized, either to supplement or to replace lack luster teachers. Children learn more about computers from their peers, and are oftentimes more familiar and comfortable with new communications and educational technologies than their teachers. It is long overdue for an overhaul of teaching university programs to revamp teaching methodologies and curriculum to reflect the reality and educational needs of our children today.

39 - EMOTIONS
[The most intensely wasted human commodity]

Everyone wants to learn ways to create, measure, and attain happiness. Some people surround themselves with people, material comforts, or pursue activities that give physical pleasure. Many people turn to sex, alcohol, and drugs to find happiness, but in the end, they become sad (which is spelled by the first letters of sex, alcohol, and drugs). Others look to escapism, extremist activities, or religion to fulfill their emotional need for happiness; but instead find disappointment in life's routines and become more unhappy because they are not able to remain in the emotional states that could be found in these types of activities.

As it was once said, "no man is an island" and we are all to a greater or lesser degree interdependent upon each others for our survival. We all live among others in communities large and small and come into contact with people on a daily basis. Other people affect how we feel about ourselves, our perceptions, expectations, happiness, or unhappiness.

Emotions appear to respond to various stimuli, including thoughts and beliefs, fears, desires, and reactions to the biochemistry of our bodies, or reaction to the words and deeds of other people. At times, we are overwhelmed by the interaction of emotional stimuli and we become depressed, confused, frustrated, angry, or may be driven to violent acts. We seek help from people who are close to us, understanding from strangers, and advice from counselors and psychiatrists. We attempt to understand our emotions, all in one or two tries, but we have little information to turn to.

Have we made inventories of the experiences and other emotional stimuli that seem to affect our level of contentment? Can we turn to personal insights, analysis, and inventories of our feelings and emotional development to give us a basis for realistically solving our emotional dilemmas? How can we expect others and professionals to figure us out, to give us life changing advice, if we have not already done the basic homework of knowing ourselves? Without our basic self-knowledge, we would in effect be asking others to send our jet plane to a desired destination, but without pinpointing the exact location of the plane at the present time. If we know where the plane had been only moments prior to the radar going out, we may extrapolate a reasonably close proximity to its actual position. Our emotional states sometimes fall off radar, and we feel lost. Referring back to emotional navigational maps that have charted our progress to date helps us to home in, so our calls for help will enable others to respond in an effective manner, as quickly as possible.

40 - ENVIRONMENTAL POLLUTION
[Forcing our children to breath, drink, and eat poison]

Natural pollution is biodegradable, usually serving to revitalize an important part of the ecosystem. Animal excrements serves as organic nutrients to replenish biochemicals in the soil, that permits plants to grow, which in turn feeds the animals. Wildfires burn away brush, weeds, and trees, leaving organic remains and pristine landscape for new seedlings to grow and flourish. But man-made pollution from the industries and cities dump billions of tons of toxic chemical wastes that pollute water, air, and soil for centuries, rendering the habitat unsafe for plants, fish, fowl, animals, and humans, especially babies and the elderly.

Industrialized nations have only recently in the past decade began to legislate more effective restrictions against industrial pollution; however, the explosive growth of cities has created monumental trash dumps that tower into the sky. Developing nations have rarely dealt with increasing environmental damage, as their short term economic and monetary interests are priority, while long-term pollution is ignored. New biotechnologies that utilize bacteria to break down various forms of chemical pollutants is still an infant industry, and effective but safe products won't be available on a large scale for another decade.

Long-term cellular and DNA damage to fetuses and children resulting from environmental pollution manifests as cancer and other diseases in adulthood that decrease the quality of health and lifespan. Due to the fact that rivers, air, and underground aquifers do not respect national boundaries, the pollution from one nations usually affects the ecology of its neighbors. Until all of the nations of the world unite and work together to reduce pollution, all humans are threaten.

41 - EMPLOYMENT
[Teach a man to fish, then give him a job]

The shrinking global economy has greatly magnified the vacillations in employment opportunities, causing drastic and sudden curtailments in certain fields while creating new opportunities in other fields, including the creation of virgin fields.

Individuals need to have a wider diversity of skills and knowledge in order to compete in the economy, as periodic job changes will continue to be the usual career track during a person's lifetime. Employment will continue to reflect global changes in the economies of member nations in various trade agreements, being affected by investor driven economic bases which respond to political stability or instability, which affects the confidence in the monetary system of the respective nations.

A balance exist between mass consumer markets and employment levels. The workers who produce manufactured goods become themselves end-use consumers, while simultaneously generating spin-off economies that are involved in the sales and marketing of the products. The laws of supply and demand dictate the delicate balance that exist between the ability of workers to afford purchases, and the level of production. If relatively high unemployment exists, markets for goods decreases, as people have less money to spend on non-subsistence products.

As the market shrinks for manufactured goods, more people become unemployed, thus exacerbating the cycle of non-productivity. Unfortunately, most greedy corporate executives fail to recognize that their own profits depend in large part on providing jobs to create a stable work force that can afford to purchase the products of industry. Henry Ford, the automotive pioneer recognized this basic principle... it takes money to buy things; and people will not have money if they don't have jobs. He realized that he could not earn a sustained profit, if he couldn't keep his own workers employed. What goes around comes around.

[Please make your complaints in writing]

Everyone has certain things that they feel strongly about. They develop strong opinions about various issues, whether it has to do with interpersonal relations, morality, politics, or religion. People often argue about various emotionally charged topics, only to find that with the passing of time, most will eventually vary their opinions from their original positions.

There are many things that people feel strongly about, sometimes intense enough to die or kill for. We all feel a sense of humanity for the sufferings of innocent children. We feel the horror of the wanton killing of people during times of war, or the perverted and senseless acts of murderers, criminals, and terrorists who reside among us. We all share a very imperfect world.

Writing essays serve to organize thoughts, offering catharsis and release of frustration at one's inability to change the negative outcomes of other people's actions. A multitude of problems need to be resolved through social awareness and political action. Many solutions abound. If more people would make their feelings known, others would be provoked to think about issues that may effect the quality of life in their communities. It is important to know what people believe about the issues that affect their lives. Too often through apathy, we obtain the type of lives and government that we deserve because we leave a void that is avidly filled by special interests. As a result, special interests have utilized government to manipulate the laws to their benefit, often to the misfortune of average citizens.

43 - EXTERNAL REALITY

[Is it real, or just in your mind?]

External events affect both our physical (external) and emotional (internal) states. Reality occurs, then we perceive, interpret, and respond to reality through our mental-emotional processes. Sometimes our fantasies and dreams appear to be real; who knows what perceptual realities are experienced by people in comas? External reality is objective, while internal reality is subjective, and varies in degree on its accurate assessment of the real world.

A person can sit in front of a computer every day during his waking hours, to sleep, then to wake and repeat the cycle all over again. It would appear to others to be a virtual reality; however, the computer world may become more real than the world outside of his room. Try to convince the person that his computer reality is not real, and there is ample argument to contend that through the computer, a person has access to information from all over the globe; consequently allowing a broader and more realistic assessment of real time reality than a person could ever obtain from leaving his computer.

Aren't our personal realities little more than perception of external stimuli that we receive through our five senses? Our informational processing system, the mind, then filters and selects particular bits of data that is needed for us to make inferences, deductions, ideas, thoughts, and conclusions. Consequently, personal reality is subject to individual perception and interpretation, thus people can create whatever reality they might choose. Even a starving person can choose to believe that they are well-fed, despite the pangs of hunger. They can go into a weakened physical state, where in a near coma trance, their mind could conjure imagery of a better reality. Naturally, it would be more humane in this instance for the person to be well fed, so the perceived realities of the observers could be consistent with the perceived reality of the observed.

44 - FAMILY VALUES
[Our parents until the end of their lives; our children until our end]

The nuclear family becomes less defined as family roles deteriorate into confusion, often culminating in broken homes and divorce. Without continuity, children are not able to observe and incorporate into their character positive moral and family values that celebrate the nuclear family and its members. As children and teens are deprived of regular positive examples of interrelational communication, sharing, love, and constructive problem solving techniques, they become dysfunctional as adults and parents since they have not adequately learned how families could function as positive and nurturing environments.

The primary causes for the break-down of the nuclear family includes socio-economic pressures that encourage both parents to compete in the work place. No longer is it possible for single-income families to enjoy a middle-class lifestyle that includes home ownership; therefore, mothers are forced into the workplace. Parents come home from work and are tired or stressed out, and make less patient and effective parents and role models for their children. Children are often left alone after school, and raise each other as peers on the playground or streets.

The television and computer becomes their surrogate parents, and most learn more from these media than from parents and schools combined. There are few programs on mass media that exemplifies family values, but instead overemphasize sex and violence within a context of drug abuse. We are what we eat and what we think. And so goes another generation, into the unknown...

45 - FEAR
[The greatest conqueror of all time]

Where did fear begin? Perhaps it is an inherited emotion, like anger and love. Without the inherited emotion of fear, the human species would have become easy prey to more ferocious wild beasts. Fear lets people be reminded of their frailty and mortality, and caused them to respect others. Those individuals who are truly fearless are socio-paths who most likely prey on others, without guilt. Fear leads to a development of compassion and conscience. All fear is not bad in and of itself. It's only when the degree of fear incapacitates the ability to act within social norms, or to attempt actions that are beneficial, do we then feel conquered by it. We have nothing to fear, but fear that incapacitates rather than motivates people to take constructive actions.

Activity defeats fear and brings out the courage from within, while inaction feeds fear due to the anxiety of contemplating bad outcomes. Is the dare devil or murderer simply courageous or perhaps it's an attempt to disguise their fear of being potential cowards? Does a lack of conscience conquer fear, or does it disguise the fear to feel afraid? In admitting one's fears, a person takes the first steps to overcome its power. In fear avoidance or denial, one succumbs to its power by acting to disguise its effects.

46 - FOLLOWERS
[The easy road is already paved by others]

People tend to be followers because there is an appearance of safety and security in the masses. There is the abrogation of personal judgment and responsibility in going along with a group. When the group benefits, all followers benefit. Should the group error, then the followers are absolved of responsibility, because, after all, they were just following the leaders, who should suffer the fate of erroneous judgments.

Following appears to be motivated by emotional needs fulfillment, while non-followers tend more to use intellectual evaluation. The leader types receive emotional strength from people's willingness to be led, giving them a false position and feeling of control and influence. Once people develop the habits of following, leaders are able to exert and intensify control through various psychological and emotional means, including threat of punishment or ridicule, or threatening to withdraw group benefits, or expulsion from the group. Those who respond to such ploys are natural born followers.

Is there more joy to being a blind follower, or does knowledge that demands individual responsibility create an undue burden that people should not have to shoulder? Should we have a society of sheep, who follow the social order, graze and move unquestionably as directed by its shepherd? Or should we build a society of brilliance, where the responsibility to forge an idyllic society is actively embraced by all of its participants?

47 - FOREIGN POLICY
[Why can't we all just get along?

Unfortunately, we all share the same world. We all compete for the same resources, and we all add our pollution to the earth, the air, the oceans, lakes, and rivers. We are stuck together on this minor planet on the edge of the Milky Way galaxy, a lesser galaxy that is more than 10 billion years away from the center of the universe.

As humans, we glorify our existence. We feel superior to all creatures that walk, fly, swim, and crawl on this planet. We ban together in groups, then we look for differences to divide our group from those who surround us. We protect our territories, but those groups who have greed for more use force to take from their close neighbors. Might made right. Colonialism, slavery, and conquest were once the inalienable rights of kingdoms and empires. To the conqueror belonged the spoils. People were commodities, owned by the rulers.

Now, we share a shrunken world proliferated with nuclear weapons, and the bomb that explodes in the neighbor's house would destroy several adjacent homes. The independent actions of single nations do impact the interests of other nations, so how do we share the world? Our governments negotiate for peace and trade, thus prosperity. The wealthy class whose interests are the mandate of governments want the world to last, so their fortunes

88

may endure. They don't want to see their fine lives and prosperity end with nuclear holocaust, overpopulation, or environmental pollution. We're fortunate that the technology doesn't yet exist for the wealthy to leave the earth for greener pastures; otherwise, they might just blow things up and start over somewhere else.

48 - FREEDOM
[Too much of a good thing?]

What is freedom? Does it mean the right to do whatever a person wants, without regards to consequences and outcomes? Now, were it possible to splice a gene into the human species to extinguish the destructive and selfish tendencies inherent to people, then there could be less concern about consequences, since everyone's actions would be the benefit of others, resulting mostly in positive outcomes. But even in a perfect world scenario, with the great variances in human beings, there would still exist competing needs that would eventually create and foster conflict.

Freedom is a balance, a compromise between competing needs that permit the least interference of government into the daily affairs of its citizens. The obstacles to higher degrees of freedom occur when some people attempt to control the affairs of others, even though the interests of others may have no affect and does not compete with their own interests. Busy bodies. People who claim to have the moral high ground. People who have not walked in another's shoes, who have no understanding or empathy for other's plights; yet feel compelled to control everyone's lives according to their own preconceived dictates. Freedom should answer to but one test; if one's actions do not have a negative affect on anyone else, then it's no one else's business.

Let freedom ring throughout the land. Let not the freedom of any one group of people enslave the freedoms of another, because if there is even one human being shackled to the state, then none of us are free. Every criminal or political incarceration decreases the expectation of freedom by changing the attitude of the public to accept a lesser degree of freedom in exchange for an illusion of a safer society. But every prison that is built further enslaves society. And the problems that create criminal behavior remains unchanged.

Freedom comes at the price of sacrifice. Freedom means that society must place responsible behavior as the end outcome of all of its institutions, from school rooms to the board rooms; from entertainment to recreation, from the churches to the bureaucratic agencies, and from the dining room to the bedroom. When mutual respect and consideration is not practiced, then freedom can not prevail; then freedom is just a word when there is nothing left to lose.

49 - FUTURE
[Stepping into the unknown]

We all want to believe that the next day will come... that there will be a future. We would want a future because we want to enjoy the things and people that surround our lives. We want a future to have chances to accomplish and experience our goals and fantasies. As the sun sets today, we all want a future in hopes of a better day, tomorrow. We want our children to have a better future than ours.

What if our life span were but 10 years after puberty? Contracting HIV at the age of 13, to die at age 23? What if our lives were no longer than those of dogs? To die at age 15? Many people are faced with these scenarios. What future do they have? Will they see their children grow up? Will they live to enjoy their grandchildren?

Sure, in a twinkle of the eye, life on earth can become extinct. An asteroid, meteor, or comet could strike the earth tomorrow. Nuclear war could begin without warning. An airborne plague could kill all humans within weeks. We can not know the future for sure. We guess at it's course, yet we do not see the greatest changes that happen before its time comes. Then, there's not much we can do about it. We react from our survival instinct, from self-preservation, selfishness, and fear. We look for benefits, and try to avoid losses, but we can't guarantee future.

50 - GREED

[Take whatever you can hold]

Before the invention of money as a medium of trade credits, people exchanged property value for value. A sheep for some chickens and blankets, for instance. The wealthy people could amass many sheep or have warehouses of blankets. But after using several blankets, and eating some chickens and sheep, there was little need to have an excess of anything one could neither use nor eat.

Once money was invented, wealth was in the land and the people that were controlled by kings, emperors, and rulers. Rulers demanded the toil, crops, animals, and property of their subjects. Silver, gold, gems, and taxes were hoarded by the rich and powerful, backed by their private armies. As archaic patriarchal authoritarian civilizations demised, to be replaced by more representative forms of government, the economic elite became the new de facto rulers. Money begets money. It's a vicious cycle. Doggy dog. Many people measure their successes and that of the people they meet by the amount of property that they own, and the size of their bank balances and stock portfolios. There is little respect given to kind and humble persons with little money.

51 - HAPPINESS
[Euphoria or fleeting moments in time?]

Think of your happiest moments. Did it cost large sums of money? It was probably free. It came unexpectedly as kindness and recognition from another human being. Or it came as self-appreciation for having earned acclaim or reaching cherished goals and expectations. Happiness is felt as an internal warmth and glow that fills the void at the pit of one's stomach. It is the feeling of elation and joy that raises one's spirit and caused one's heart to flutter and fly. Happiness usually corresponds directly to fulfillment of personal expectations, or the expectations of others that result in recognition and praise. Sometimes, happiness comes from acquiring property and gifts, or from spiritual awareness. It is a subjective phenomenon that usually involves positive events; however, negative outcomes can create euphoria in some people, who may enjoy inflicting pain and torment in others.

Excitement, contentment, fulfillment, and peace of mind are elements or outcomes of happiness. Happiness results when the brain sends out electrical impulses to the responding trigger points in the emotional command center portion of the brain in reaction to biochemical changes that occur in our sensory receptors, coupled with conditioned response protocols that we both inherited and learned. That's why individuals respond differently to similar situations, sometimes feeling elated, but at other times expressing frustration or unhappiness. Combined, sensory stimuli, perception, conditioned response, programming, bio-chemistry, heredity, and mentation interact in a complex web to give a feeling of happiness, or lack thereof.

52 - HATRED
[Extreme self-love]

It is sometimes said that love and hate are the same feeling, but on the extreme ends of the same spectrum. How does a married couple who were brought together by intense love, eventually divorce each other with extreme hatred? How is it possible to hate someone who was the object of such profound love, that one would have sacrificed their own life to preserve that of another? Then to hate that person so deeply that thoughts of murder spontaneously fill the heart and mind.

Perhaps people confuse unselfish, unconditional love for other human beings with the selfish, self-serving love of oneself. People profess love for others, as long as others return self-ingratiating benefits. Material, physical, sexual, and monetary benefits all contribute to the development of desire, which is interpreted as love. Consequently, if the benefits are withdrawn, then the feelings of love turn to hatred. People rationalize and blame others for committing injustices; when in actuality, others are simply withdrawing their contribution of various desired benefits. Is that deserving of hatred? A person gives twenty years of love, consideration, gifts, etc., but decides to reduce the level of giving, then becomes the object of hate. Were's the love?

53 - HEREDITY
[Hardwired programming]

Anyone who has had experience raising or teaching children notices that no two persons are exactly alike, with the exception of identical twins who are almost perfectly similar in physical appearance, innate intelligence, and talents to each other. We find personality variations among identical twins because no two persons are ever treated exactly alike by their parents; and as separate individual occupying separate space and life journeys, significant differences will be evident due to a multitude of environmental factors.

Theoretically, identical twins who are raised exactly alike, and are exposed to the exact same environmental stimuli at the same time, may develop sameness in personality, talents, abilities, attitudes, and thoughts. Identical twins who have spent much time together will often anticipate what the other twin will say, before it is spoken. There may be a strong psychic connection between these twins, such that one can actually feel the other's emotions and "know" what the other one is thinking about in general terms in certain situations.

The science of cloning presents unique opportunities for studying the effects of DNA on the range of inheritable traits. Besides the obvious physical attributes, what else appears to be primarily outcomes of DNA? Can genotyping become accurate predictors of criminal behavior, social adaptability, genius, athleticism, artistic talent, or humanitarianism? And once having identified and correlated genotype to predispositioned mentality, emotionality, and behavior, would society embark on choosing to eliminate or to promote certain genes. Would Hitler's dream of a superior race be derived through science, what could not be forced on the world through war?*

54 - HONESTY
[The truth hurts]

If people were to speak their minds, and be one hundred percent honest in their actions all of the time, two things would happen. First, the devious people who control society, economies, and governments would no longer be in power. Secondly, after a drawn out period of conflict in people's everyday relations, if they are still standing, there would be a greater mutual respect for people's differences than ever before in the history of human civilizations.

People are raise in most cultures to hide the truth, and to show only what may bring oneself benefits, honor, praise, and approval. Honesty is preached by adults to their children, but deceit is the daily order of events in the adult world. How many people would voluntarily report themselves to the police for every time that they exceeded the speed limit, or slowly rolled past a stop sign so they could pay the fine, and exercise their civic responsibility to make the streets safer? How often will people admit to their spouses that they were committing adultery? And isn't it common for people to flatter another, when in fact, they may not believe their own words, just to gain or maintain a relationship?

The things people normally tell the truth about are usually mundane and do not have potentially negative consequences. People will tell the truth about foods that they eat at restaurants, but may lie if prepared by close friends or relatives. People will admit the time that they awake and the time that they sleep if the admission would give the impression of success and not laziness. They will tell you the time of day, if it is raining outside their house, or if the sun is out. There usually is no beneficial motive to mislead others on these mundane facts. But women will lie to men whether they enjoyed a sexual encounter. And men will tell women that they are in love if it enhances their chances of getting sex.

People will put all their money into nice clothes and a car, and have little else to show, but the superficial appearance stands to deceive others into believing that nice clothes and car equates to social and monetary success. It is only after people are able to shed the judgmental aspects of their socialization, and to accept themselves for what they are, and to accept others for being diversely different; then and only then would honesty become the common ground in communication and interaction. Most people need to develop and practice honesty in their daily lives, without being mean spirited. Telling the truth in nice and considerate ways can be an empowering and freeing phenomenon.

A person who focuses on noble intentions will have little problem in telling the truth; while those with hidden selfish agendas, who are enamored by seeking self-serving desirable outcomes, will act as if they are being truthful, but instead are engaged in deceit.

55 - HUMAN NATURE
[Our ancestors made us do it]

The inherited portion of emotionality is defined as basic human nature. All people possess primary instincts for survival, protection of their young, procreation, and fight or flight in the face of danger. Social development and the creation of rules of conduct has added layers of complexity and deceit to our natural instincts and drives, creating a confusing state of affairs. People find it difficult to recognize or admit what is natural, and what is societal. The desire to build or to destroy; to escape or accept responsibility;

to seek security and love; to express anger, jealousy, and hatred; to make excuses and blame others for failures and wrong-doings; and the need to seek acceptance and to obtain approval are all part of our human make-up. But how much is a part of our human nature?

If we accept the fact that human behavioral propensities are inherited as part of the written code in the DNA, then we must realize humans possess both the desire to act negatively and selfishly. Children are not born as blank slates, with the desire to do good. Humans are born inherently self-serving, and possess the innate capacity to commit both benevolent as well as heinous acts.

One of the greatest challenges to people in civilized societies is the recognition and acceptance of the importance of the common good over individual needs. Were everyone to act on their human nature, anarchy would reign, as the strong would defeat the weak. The primal human tendency is to rape, pillage, and destroy. We need look no further than any of recent human conflicts, or wars to see the flagrant degradation of the human spirit as people are wantonly killed, tortured, raped, and dehumanized, all for the rights and benefits of a select group of individuals or demagogic leaders.

It is through the course of enlightenment, and true universal love for others that humans are able to restrain their natural tendencies to destroy others, their environment, and all living things. Humans are not good by nature, but instead, must learn to behave constructively.

56 - HUMANISM
[Saving ourselves from ourselves]

Humans are the only species of animals that regularly commits violence on its own members, occasionally practicing genocide. Animals prey on other animals for food, but not on its own kind. Humans, supposedly with intellect vastly superior to all other creatures, exhibits base emotions and behavior more ferocious than nature's most formidable carnivores. Were it not for the influence of more enlightened people, the masses of people would likely beat each other into anarchy.

Imagine a world as an armed camp, without laws, without organization and justice. Could we trust people to do the right thing? Or would the most vicious and deviant members intimidate and develop power to subjugate, enslave, and murder the weaker members? The history of human civilizations is filled with dictators, who as rulers, have killed untold millions of innocent men, women, and children. Hitler gassed and burned 8 million Jews; Pol Pot butchered and buried alive over 6 million Cambodian subjects over whom he ruled; Stalin put untold millions into death camps; Mao-Tse-Tung unleashed disruptive programs that resulted in the hard labor imprisonment and death of countless millions of people, and our own government directed the U.S. Calvary to chase and reduce the Native American population from over 50 million to less than 100,000 at the end of the Indian wars. And in the last two major world wars, over 100 million people lost their lives, in addition to 25 million military personnel.

Humans are our own worst enemy. There exist no other creature on earth that is a threat or enemy of mankind. Despite overpopulation of the planet, inhumanity can not be justified as a sane method of population control. Each life that is disrespected, harmed, abused, or destroyed denigrates civilization and the collective human spirit. Each act of inhumanity that is tolerated reduces the humanity that remains in all of us. When people become desensitized to murder and rape, as it is glamorized and depicted as part of mass entertainment, our quality of life decreases, as the emotionally unstable copycat followers find purpose in acting out more insanity.

57 - ILLUSIONS
[Smoke and mirror realities]

When people look into a mirror, they see reflected back a likeness of the exterior appearance of themselves. As people interact with their environments, they develop a set of operating principles, perceptual filters, and illogical self-serving rationalizations as methods to protect their sense of self-worth. People often lie to themselves. Like in the Disney classic, SNOW WHITE, the evil queen persona seeks to be the most beautiful, reflecting an insecurity that pervades her behavioral motives. And like the story, people often attempt to criticize, sabotage, denigrate, or even to murder those whom they feel are obstacles or threats to their sense of self-worth. They wish to hold on to the illusion, that they are fairest in their perceived world.

If we look closer at the dynamics of self-worth and relationships, it becomes obvious that most processes and perceptions are illusory. Most people deal with themselves and others as if they were looking at reflections, and not the real entities. People speak, act, and appear certain ways to fit in to their perceived expectations of what is acceptable or admirable among their peers, whether at work, church, or in social settings. Sometimes so many mirrors are used, that finding the true person is like getting trapped in the house of mirrors. Except that in an amusement park's "fun house", people can exit the "house of mirrors" and back into reality. It is much more difficult when people's reality is the illusion.

58 - IMPORTANCE
[What makes it so urgent?]

The lone actions of one Luke Skywalker sets into motion a series of reactions that saves the universe from the dark forces of destruction. That's damn important! A child is struck by a truck, and lies in a pool of blood, as the life force oozes out onto the pavement. People frantically attempt to resuscitate the child.

That's urgent! The boss throws another tantrum because he has set an unreasonable deadline, and the report is not yet on his desk. That's ridiculous. However, many people would feel pressured and stress from irrational employers who have personality problems. People react to priorities set by the demands of others, whether they are bosses, government bureaucrats, or friends and family. If people were to set their own priorities, they would gain a greater sense of peace.

What is really so important in life? Being on time on one's wedding day? Getting to the bank, post office, or shopping mall sale when they first open the doors? Dropping your tax forms off by midnight on April 15th? Getting a babysitter to come over to watch the children, so a night out for entertainment would be possible? Hoping the dinner that on the stove will be delicious to the guests? People have a distorted sense of importance. That's why there's so much crime. Collectively, the shapers of society have decided that activities related to earning or saving money is important, and everything else can wait. We place less priority on providing food to starving children, better homes and schools, and meaningful jobs to our citizens.   Cities are blighted by the homeless, gangs, and violence. And while politicians talk about solutions, it's not important enough to spend the money on them.

59 - INDIVIDUALITY

[Self-discovery and emergence]

Those   who do not conform to social definitions and expectations are seen as outcasts or iconoclasts who fall outside of the range of social norms, including those for appearance, behavior, and speech. Nonconformist are viewed by others as being weird. Individualists do not behave in expected ways to gain social acceptance. They don't care what the average follower thinks.   Does Michael Jackson, the King of Pop, seek people's approval of his idiosyncrasies? Were it not for the creative non-conformists, everyday would be another McDonald's hamburger day, with a soda and fries.   There would be little social, philosophical, or technological progress without individualists.

The non-conformists are often ahead of their times. Typically, their ideas and views are first shunned, then ridiculed by the upholders of the status quo, so called leaders and their mass followers; only later to embrace as trendy or mainstream the same odd notions that were rejected decades in the past. Clothing, hairstyles, rituals, customs, and speech patterns once ridiculed become the item of the month a few years later, when the public finds it fanciful to copy individualistic trend-setters.

60 - INTERNAL
[Secret motives and lives]

What you see is usually not what you get. Take cereal packages for instance. The fancy box shows deliciously colored product that is blown up to cause an emotional impulsive response to buy. But once the box is opened, the contents only resemble the packaging. The amount of real food content and nutritional value is rarely worth the purchase price. People are like cereal boxes. Make-up, clothing, hairstyle, the smile, the gait, the car, the credit cards, the bank account, the decorated home, the personality and charm, all to create a desire in the potential consumer. But once the car is garaged, the clothing and make-up comes off, the theatrical personality is off stage, and the bank balance is not available, people are confronted with the contents of what is really beyond the packaging. And what is on the inside usually only resembles the outside.

The main reason people don't get along is that what they bought into isn't really who they thought they would get most of the time. People do not show their hidden motives and secret agendas until a customer has been sucked into the trap. People live secret lives, hoping not to be discovered. Brilliant students during the day, but prostitutes or hoodlums during the night. Successful corporate executive by day, and obnoxious drunk by night. Admired entertainer, but cocaine addict. Powerful politician or government bureaucrat by day, but cross dresser by night. Prostitutes love political and religious conventions because some of their best customers are conservative pillars of their local communities, but sexual deviates when not under close scrutiny to live up to their rhetoric. If wives only knew a tenth of what prostitutes know about their husband's secret lives, divorce lawyers would have guaranteed life time employment. And that's not to exonerate wives, many, who like in "Valley of the Dolls", also lead secret lives.

61 - JEALOUSY
[Ultimate insecurity]

Is it possible and permissible for a person to enjoy tennis, but also love skydiving. Or to spend time polishing his car, but to admire the polished look of a Harley Davidson motorcycle? Is it acceptable for people to care about their parents, children, relatives, friends, and lovers, all at the same time? It is within the human

104

potential to have more than one romantic interest simultaneously? The answer is a resounding "yes" in each case. Then why do people show much irrational jealousy when they are "the other" lover or friend? Does spending time, money, and affection on another person automatically make a person an evil, bad, and untrustworthy? Must we accept the premise that similar well intentioned actions that are directed at two different persons is bad, but if focused on one person, it is good? That irrationality is the basis of jealousy.

Jealousy is insecurity, surrounded by greed. Why must a person want all of someone's attention and affection? Is this possessiveness of another person's love, jealousy, an innate human trait? Perhaps it is so, that during the formative years of human evolution, the intense desire to possess another, flamed by jealousy, permitted more assertive members to succeed in procreation in greater numbers. Consequently, the human propensity toward unreasonable jealousy has been selectively bred into the species. Survival of the fittest. Fortunately, we humans have long progressed past that era of Neanderthal behavior, or have we? Perhaps jealousy is just another negative emotional trait that reacts to environmental and perceptual stimuli, that humans must purge in its journey toward peace and enlightenment. Hate, greed, deceit, violence, and jealousy have greatly impeded the evolution of humans into their full potential as intelligent and contributing entities in the cosmos.

62 - JUSTICE

[Just ice... cold hard facts, or what?]

Justice is supposed to be impartial. Justice is supposed to be blind. Justice is supposed to be fair. However, in the pursuit of justice, we find society falls short more often than it seems to score a bull's-eye. How many guilty criminals now run the streets, continuing their reign of terror on the innocent? And how many innocent people are locked in societies of terror, convicted of crimes they did not commit because politicians, district attorneys, and law enforcement want to improve their personal conviction rates? Why can a wealthy person find loop holes in the law, while the working class and impoverished find only holes in their pockets? Where's the equal justice?

The justice system is imperfect, but that doesn't mean we should accept imperfection as the nature of the beast. The justice system does not emphasize the search for the truth; but instead it is a battleground between the careers of attorneys and government prosecutors, each vying to embellish their own credentials and scorecards. The O.J. Simpson trial clearly demonstrated to the world the arcane adversary nature of the American justice system. What ever happened to the primary pursuit of justice, the search for the truth? Why has it become a side show that relies on untrained members of the public, with their own hidden biases and agendas, to evaluate technical and scientific data, to make life and death judgments on the lives of the accused? Perhaps if the proponents of our legal system spent more time searching for truth, and less time worrying about their careers, we could make the system work.

Otherwise, let's change the law, and subject all accused people to a series of truth revealing tests, such as polygraph, voice stress analysis, and truth-serum. But, trial lawyers would be against anything that violates their need for more customers. Which is the worse evil, allowing the state to test people's honesty, or to allow criminals to roam free, while some innocent people are locked up?

63 - LAWS
[Forcing conformity on conformist]

Laws made from the self-interests of law-makers protect certain special interest groups or classes of people while unfairly punishing other groups at large. Who are our law-makers really serving? What are their motivations? The laws are only as good as the intentions. If we wish to control or encourage certain forms of public behavior, do we really need another punitive law? Wouldn't we be more effective to teach our children common sense, respect for the rights of others, consideration, and honesty? Laws should be guidelines that define the range of acceptable public behavior. Laws should not invade people's right to privacy, the right to speak or act in ways that may not conform to the norm, just so long as it is kept private, and does not intrude on the rights of others.

Too often, we find our politicians legislating morality, religiosity, and philosophy. If a person wants to jump out of an airplane without a parachute onto an empty field, why should government intervene? If a person wants to walk the streets stark naked, why shouldn't people just turn their heads if they don't like what they see? More people would probably laugh at the sight of a naked person than would complain about its apparent indecency. Why should government be in the business of telling its citizens how many spouses they can have simultaneously? Government is becoming too invasive and pervasive. Cameras are everywhere, along with hidden microphones. The Cornelian nightmare is upon us, and most people just accept it. The next phase is a Brave New World that is less than a decade away.

64 - LEADERS
[Leading the flock away from the herd]

In the absence of leaders, left to their own design, most people would naturally communicate and make beneficial alliances and agreements. Add the leader, and after a while the group's interest begins to conform to the needs of the leader. People relinquish their responsibility to make rational decisions, and instead defer themselves to follow leaders. It's not the nature of people to be blind followers, but rather it is natural for people to want to trust in others. Leaders take advantage of people's trust, for good or for bad. When leaders take actions to benefit their followers, in direct response to their real needs, then leadership has the potential to shine, and human progress continues. In times when leaders used their followers to support megalomaniac fantasies, the outcome is usually massive wars of destruction, such as those fought in the name of Adolph Hitler, and various kings, czars, khans, sultans, and emperors down through human history.

Leaders tend to rejoice in their own significance and importance. After bathing in adoration and over consumption of their apparent control over the masses, they want to separate their group from those who may not be in their flock. They create slogans, banners, and apparel for their followers, so they can spot and round up their sheep from the vast herd. Leaders want to have a following that they can call their own. They want a head count, to bathe in the knowledge of knowing how many human lives have been sacrificed to follow their bidding. Who invented leadership? Why is it so difficult for grown people to sit down to discuss issues, then to take a vote, then to agree on a course of action that is binding? Why does it take a parent/leader to get people to do those things they all know needs to be done? Human beings are still children in terms of emotional development, acting on irrationality, impulsiveness, primal desires, and monetary motivation. When will the species evolve to the point that they can stand as equals before each other, and to resolve the problems of their time without the need to rely on leaders? Without a need for leaders, the problem of being misled disappears, doesn't it?

65 - LIES
[Not the opposite of honesty]

Being untruthful is not simply the opposite of honesty. Honesty does not take intent or effort. Honesty is just being factual. Dishonesty, however, has the added component of insidious intent. To know the truth, then to lie, can not be innocent and accidental. Lying is a deliberate attempt to deceive other people for purposeful gain and self-benefits. Consequently, dishonesty is a ploy and a strategy to disarm trusting people, so that benefits which may otherwise not be offered may be obtained through manipulation.

In today's complex societies, people routinely lie to avoid losses, or to improve their potential gain. People even lie to "protect" others from knowing the truth, to avoid hurting people with the truth. This line of reasoning is not logical, but is an attempt to rationalize acts that were mistakes, errors, or problematic. Why do people need to be protected from the truth? Let's take the case of an adulterous spouse. In the long-term, isn't it better for both people in a marriage to face sexual infidelity as a fact, so each person may exercise free choice in accepting, rejecting, or correcting the behavior? The adulterous person feels compelled to lie, to keep the truth hidden, for fears of losing a benefit of the existing marriage. The potential outcome, divorce, and other economic and familial losses is more important to the adulterer than in being truthful. This motivation for lying, concealment, is very common in people's daily lives. That's why trust is a concept that is rapidly being replaced by caution, skepticism, and distrust.

66 - LIFE
[It should come with a money back guarantee]

People are born into this world with no guarantees. They were conceived usually as the outcome of the pleasure their genetically-linked parents had during sexual intercourse. There was usually no planning of the type of life parents would try to give to their offsprings. Children in most parts of the world, including American inner-cities are born into lives of hopelessness, despair, and suffering. We need look no further than the atrocious conditions in most nations during recent history to see great inhumanity and suffering.

If life came with a money-back guarantee, most people would be wealthy by the time of retirement. Instead, the vast majority, over 90 percent of retirees rely on government assistance and are essentially broke. The world has abundant resources to clothe, shelter, and feed all of its inhabitants, if only the wealth of the earth were more fairly shared with those who toil to create it. The value of all the products, cities, and crops of current civilizations is around $1,000,000,000,000,000. If there were a way to redistribute the wealth to earth's 5.5 billion people in more or less equal proportions, each man, woman, and child would have about $180,000, which certainly would eliminate hunger and most diseases related to poor sanitation, insufficient habitat, and malnourishment. Every child that is born should be entitled to at the least, the bare essentials necessary for a healthy life. Otherwise, the greedy hoarding minority of wealthy people should have to pay the poor people for the sufferings of their miserable impoverished lives.

67 - LONGEVITY
[Still way short of immortality]

Folklore, mythology, religion, and fantasy all mention human's desire to achieve immortality. Ponce deLeon, sailed off into the unknown in his search for the "Fountain of Youth" during which he died looking, but never finding. Perhaps in death, this explorer fulfilled his life long journey, and forever remains young in another dimension. People have been forever looking for ways to remain youthful, and to extend their lives. The Bible states that Adam, Moses, and other early holy men lived almost 1,000 years.

But recorded history can not verify any one living beyond 120 years, which appears to be the upper limit of the human lifespan. However, scientific studies in the fields of genetics and pharmacology indicates the possibility that the lifespan of human beings could be extended to at least 150 years in the near future. What would the quality of life be once a person passes the century mark? What rejuvenation regimens would have to be employed at an early age, and what type of environmental controls would have to be in place to minimize the debilitating effects of aging bodies?

Could it be possible that bacteria or viruses have something to do with causing aging? Is there a gene that could be activated in the human body to retard aging, and to increase longevity? If we look at the universality of the atomic structure, why shouldn't it be logical for physical deterioration to be related to processes that occur on sub-atomic and sub-cellular levels? Thousands of ants build an ant hill, complete with subterranean caverns; yet we see only the obvious surface structure.

What constant dynamic processes are causing aging, and what can be done to retard the process? It is common knowledge that sunlight ages the skin. Do cosmic rays cause a gradual decay of subdermal cells? Does an interactive effect of cosmic and ultraviolet radiation, chemical and organic pollutants, and bacterial and viral intrusion cause aging, decrease in functionality, and eventual death? Is immortality possible if the factors that cause cellular decay, and limit specific cellular regeneration, could be managed? Is a magic longevity pill that acts to retard aging by retarding the effects of environmental factors, while activating specific regenerative and immune system genes within the realm of possibility, or probability?

68 - LOSS
[The downside of gains]

People avoid activities or situations that presents a risk of loss. Compromise is a strategy that attempts to decrease risks and increases the probability of benefits; thus decreasing the probability of large losses. When faced with greater opposing forces, losses are accepted, or rationalized to deny the recognition of loss; rather the outcomes are explained in terms of temporary setbacks or retrenchment.

What benefits one person often comes as a loss to another. Take money, property, time, and even love, for instance and it is often observed, that one person's loss is usually another's gain. If everyone begins from zero, there would be nothing to lose; however, once individuals accrue emotional stakes in material possessions or property rights in relationships, then occasional losses are to be expected. It is in the attitude toward and perception of loss that creates a dichotomy between gains and losses. Society's overemphasis on sports, on declaring one individual or team as winner, as the best, denigrates the status of those whose noble and courageous efforts may not have resulted in the desired outcome. One winner and the rest losers. Humans have stacked the odds against winning, and assured a world of losers.

The sense of loss quite often is a matter of perspective. The tide ebbs in and out. Sunlight illuminates for a time, to be replaced by light from the moon and stars. There is no loss, only a change in scenery. People's lives are not dissimilar to the tides, sun, moon, and stars. The constant principle of change is universally operating at all levels from the sub-atomic to the galactic.

113

Every cell in the human body, and every electron in the brain is in a constant state of flux, being altered billions of times within the span of each second. There is no loss in life, merely changes in the state of the scenery. A person is fired from a job, goes on employment, and later begins another career. The apparent loss, in retrospect, becomes a point from which a change of scenery occurs. Movement is always a gain. The outcome may differ from one's expectations or goals in financial terms; however, change adds to life's experience, thus it is a gain, and not a loss. It is in the subjective assignment of positive or negative value to situations that loss is created as a judgmental concept. To the universe, a loss or gain is simply continuation of molecular motion on a macro level.

69 - LOVE
[The ultimate sacrifice]

The discussion and analysis of love has continued from ancient times to the present. Great philosophers and writers such as Socrates, Lao-Tze, Jesus Christ (as Son of God), Buddha, Mohammed, Shakespeare, and Plato have all expounded on the perpetual subject of love. Ann Rand has espoused self-love as the ultimate motive for love. Aldous Huxley defined the various types of love, from self-centered, to other-center to universal love. Love has been defined to include emotional, mental, spiritual, and physical aspects. Cultural, social, biochemical, hereditary, and economic determinants have been theorized as factors that interact to create love; but love appears to remain a fleeting concept that can not be completely defined and encapsulated.

The feeling of love is a perception. It is not possible to reach into one's pocket, pull out some love, and to give it to another (except in a physical sense). A person can tell another that they are the object of love, but the receiver may not feel it, nor accept it as a desirable offering. People tend to define a series of demonstrations as indicators that love is present. Usually, confirmation that love is present takes the form of gift giving, physical touching, sexual contact (except in regards to familial taboos), sharing of secrets, acceptance of mutual imperfections, verbal affirmations, enjoyment of mutual interests and activities, self-sacrifice, and the willingness to give up one's life to preserve the life of another.

Several models of love have been proposed, each attempting to quantify the phenomenon into descriptions such as unconditional, absolute, or universal; degrees of, object-specific, self-centered, or situational. Each category explains various apparent outcomes of love, but none are all-inclusive in communicating the emotional impact and transference of love. Love is similar to a rubber ball. It bounces around. It can be pumped up, or deflated. The external skin can be touched, and the texture felt. It can be passed back and forth. But the love inside is invisible, and people can only imagine what it must feel or appear on the inner side of the skin. When attempts are made to measure it from the inside, the ball pops, and all the air is expelled. Love can be like that. Love is a very personal emotion that can not be felt by another. Others can only imagine what someone feels when they say the three most powerful words in the universe, "I love you." People can only feel the external texture of love, and assume that the inside is at the least as sensuous. It probably is, and then much more.

70 - MUNDANE
[Being an average goat]

How many people feel excited and fulfilled about living a mundane life? People are never interviewed on television news, exclaiming that they have a happy mundane lifestyle. Boring is the first word that would normally be associated with an average mundane existence. Nothing to brag about, and probably not even worth talking about; certainly not a centerpiece of conversation. Imagine how interesting it would be to hear about a typical day at the drive in window at McDonald's, or another day writing computer programs. Sure, once in a while strange and unusually interesting situations occur at the job. Accidents do happen. Think of the tens of millions of people who spend their lives at their jobs, repeating routine mindless uninteresting tasks. That's why people seek escapist and recreational activities, to feel thrill, excitement, and even danger... to feel alive, like children.

Life doesn't need to be mundane. The primary purpose of socialization is to condition conformity to ensure social order. Unfortunately, the typical outcome of schooling, church, and laws is to stamp out the thirst, excitement, and passion for life that is naturally exhibited by children under the age of 5, before acclimation to kindergarten. By the time a child graduates from grade school, individuality and self-expression is repressed, and replaced by conformity to peer and authoritarian expectations. Children are rewarded for displaying sheepishly appropriate behavior on their way to achieving a mundane existence. And once schooling is complete, and children mature into adulthood, they sheepishly accept the only lifestyle they have been taught, one filled with mundane tasks, goals, and outcomes.

How can adults regain the excitement for life? How can people feel like children, yet be able to function in a compartmentalized world that is regulated by bureaucracies, rules, and regulations? How can the unrestrained thirst for freedom of expression be rekindled in a constructive manner, that fulfills people's need to shout loudly from the innermost depths of their hearts and souls? A life with little passion is a mere existence. Life filled with opportunities to be heard and appreciated, to accomplish, to experience, and to feel elation and happiness is certainly worth waking up to daily.

71 - NICE PEOPLE
[Suckers are born every second]

The nicest and most giving persons that the majority of people will ever know in their lives are likely to be their mother and father. Nice people are those who demonstrate kindness, moral support, and empathetic understanding. Nice people usually become the security blanket for others. They also typically become taken for granted. Their acts of love and consideration become expected, unnoticed, and unappreciated. And when nice people fail to maintain the expected level of generosity, the dependents who benefited from the kindness usually become disappointed, hurt, and angered by the withdrawal. Then the nice people are branded as being unloving, inconsiderate, and selfish. But what effort has the taker made lately to support the relationship? Obviously, takers see a different reflection in their character mirror than that which is reality.

Nice people tend to have several traits in common; the desire for approval; a deficiency in feeling appreciated, admired, or loved; a need to nurture or give as a humanitarian statement of one's self-worth; and a drive to love as sacrifice of personal gains for the benefit of others. Selfish people love to enjoy the support and gains that are available from nice people; but they often do not love the generous person. Selfish people continue to pretend to like nice people, in order to ensure present and future benefits.

Nice people are often "used", and are considered as "suckers" by the very selfish people who benefit from the love and labor of nice people. The real suckers are the parasitic selfish people who feel so proud of their ability to use nice people as if they were tools or instruments for their enjoyment and self-aggrandizement. Suckers are not born every second... they are nice people whose life blood is eventually sucked out by self-serving takers. Nice people are becoming a dying breed, an endangered species. When they are gone, only the parasitic blood suckers will be left, only without an easy blood supply. They won't last long without the contributions of nice people. Nice people shoulder the burdens of the world, without whom the world would collapse on the weight of its deadbeats.

72 - PARENTING
[Do as we tell you, and not as we do]

In retrospect, most people wish they could have been better parents. Many first time parents take courses in early child development and parenting, to prepare themselves for an exciting and wonderful new addition to their lives. They seek the knowledge and a road map to raising happy and well-adjusted children. But most people find that there is a large gap between textbook and actual practice in the real world. No child is raised in a vacuum, and no child responds just as predicted in these quasi-scientific child rearing books. Often, environmental and genetic personality factors derail parents' best attempts to be the perfect parents who have perfect children.

When children are young, before they become school age, they are usually innocent, silly, and a pleasure to watch. Young children are spontaneous, funny, and generally obedient. The expression of their little lives are fresh, unpredictable, and entertaining. Then they are placed on the train that goes down the track which leads to socialization. We see them gradually lose their sense of self, and instead begin to adopt a series of behavior that more reflects the imitation of peers than expressions of their true personalities. Childhood innocence is lost as various mean spirited adults and children inflict pain on unsuspecting children. Why are some people so bad? Parents try to explain away the hurt, but all that is done is similar to placing a bandage on a cut, and allowing time for the wound to heal. In time, the bumps, cuts, and bruises heal, leaving internalized, hidden, and disguised emotional scars that may surface later in life during the teenage years or to remain unresolved as adults.

Many theological traditionalist believe "spare the rod, and spoil the child." How does one teach children to show compassion and to love each other by inflicting violence on them? Will they be able to handled physical punishment and torture without serious emotional damage that may reappear as anti-social behavior later in life? Is it a wonder that over half of all marriage end in divorce, and that some form of physical or emotional abuse is found in two-thirds of all households?

Everyone suffers during marital discountenance. But the children are powerless to effect anything. They are the helpless victims of adult inabilities or unwillingness to swallow their false pride, and to work things out as adults should do. The children look to their parents to show them how adults can effectively resolve the problems of the day, to make everything okay and happy again. A big regret expressed by many parents is that they were often not positive examples of how adults should express love in a marriage. It's no wonder many teenagers often state that they don't plan to marry or to have children. In divorced families, children often blame themselves to some extent for contributing to the friction in the home, and that in some way that cause the parents to break up.

73 - PAST EXPERIENCES
[Trial and error, learning like a mouse]

Periodic review of past accomplishments, experiences, and situations permit people to compare the state of their present lives to that which was. Recalling successes gives people significance, contentment, and happiness. Making inventory lists aids the recall of important events and feelings, and to enable the assessment of past errors. Lessons learned from past mistakes permit people to move forward, and to avoid similar traps of their past. Listing various ideas and theories that affect a person's world view helps to clarify beliefs and desires. Some sample inventories listed below have been part of most people's awareness, self-acceptance, and fulfillment: activities, alcohol mistakes, business strategies, career choices, community environments, cars, character traits, goals, habits, injuries, interests, job history, job skills, life attainments, life priorities, preferences, realities, relationships, state of life, wants, wasteful acts, wishes.

Everyone has lived different lifestyles and responded to various circumstances in their own unique ways. Some people may think of lists not mentioned here, such as vacations, sexual experiences and partners, favorite foods, health history of diseases, annual income, near death experiences, and incidents of abuse, racism or sexism. Inventory lists are personal recollections of significant events that may have altered or shaped one's life.

74 - PEOPLE
[People, people everywhere, but not one soul to link]

How one gets along with other people determines to a great extent one's self-image and the level of happiness they may experience. There are three primary types of interactive personality styles:

1. The giver, who seeks to please others in exchange for appreciation, affection, and a sense they have been a "good" person.

2. The taker, who seeks primarily to fulfill selfish needs by using others to provide what they would otherwise have to do for themselves. This style may be perceived as "dependency" or as "manipulative" as projected by a submissive versus aggressive character.

3. The dodger, who avoids involvement in seeking help, or in giving help. The perception is that dependency creates a feeling of bondage, that one owes a favor in return. And there is the realization that helping others often comes at a loss to one's own time and resources, and is usually not repaid in kind.

Most people express all three styles to varying degrees depending upon who they are dealing with, and on the situation. Generally, over the course of a week, people tend to take on one personality style over the others. There are people who tend to be nice to everyone who they meet. But they often experienced disappointment, when those who have benefited from their help find weak excuses why help would not be returned if they had a need. Fortunately, many friends and family members who have benefited will often charged aid a cherished friend during some very trying times. Oftentimes people feel "used" by acquaintances during the "feeling out" period, prior to developing a friendship. Then there are the fair weather friends, who one by one I will cause disappointment. True friends? The "real" people? They exist.

In order to become more satisfied in relationships, decide what positive attributes are desired in a person. Evaluate people with an objective standard, with emotional detachment. In addition, rate oneself against the same standards that are applied to others. Are you worthy of the type of people that you seek? Avoid the unrealistic syndrome of wanting a Mercedes on a Volkswagen budget and trying to rationalize that you deserve a Mercedes simply because you are a good person. Most people would want a Mercedes, but most people don't actually earn or deserve one.

Now, when it comes to people, feel that you deserve high quality people in your life, because you are confident that what you have to offer is comparable in value.

What do you want from people? What do you have to offer them? If you take some time to list your criteria, you may well discover that you're hanging around the wrong people, or maybe you need to do some fine tuning of your own self-worth.

75 – POLITICIANS (1995)
[The nature of power and government]

The American system of government is essentially a bureaucratic legal nightmare. The cost of running government from the federal, state, and local levels cost half of the nation's GNP, over $2.5 trillion. One out of every four jobs is work in the bureaucracy. Politicians are part-time campaigners, with one eye on the next election to the same or higher office. Their public activities and voting records are orchestrated to create sound bites for television and to make friends with special interest lobbyist. The political solutions to society's problems are usually ineffective, passing too many laws that prey on people's fears, filling prisons with dysfunctional people who need help, instead of incarceration. Politicians are uncreative control freaks, whose myopic perspective is monetary fine, property seizure, and imprisonment as the outcome of legislation. Normally law-abiding citizens are turned into criminals, and it is almost impossible to go through life without being guilty of breaking some law. Almost everything is against a law, ordinance, rule, or regulation. Everyone at sometime pays a fine to government for infraction of laws, and one-third of citizens will be jailed sometime during their lives.

Political motives are often dishonest, creating a climate of legal confusion that elates lawyers, and complicates policing functions to the point that most citizens no longer admire or respect either the laws, lawmakers, law enforcement, or the courts. The political agenda has become one of protecting government for its own sake. Government no longer exists to serve the people. Government is a creature whose purpose is self-propagation, with a mandate to control its citizens through intimidation, coercion, extortion, and punishment. People who become part of the bureaucracy conduct the affairs of government, and tend to view citizens as burdens; yet when they find themselves on the end of long lines for government services, they fail to make the connection that another uncaring government bureaucrat most likely is on a coffee break, and isn't interested in the people's business.

Politicians continue their adversarial campaign postures right into legislative country club lifestyles. They join to fight opposition grassroots groups, while they enjoy the privileges granted to their offices, which include protectionism, selective enforcement of laws that often exempt them from fines and punishment, and networking the special interest lobbies for lifestyle enhancements. They reward each other with generous perks and windfall retirement plans, all at their constituents' expense, and without taxpayers' concurrence. It's no wonder social inequities abound; racial strife, gender warfare, and violent crimes are all outcomes of political agendas and policies that do not correct the root causes of society's problems. And what incentives do politicians have to serve the people, to solve long standing decay in the socio-economic fabric of their communities? If the problems go away, why would society need politicians? What emotionally charged issues would be left for political platforms?

76 - POOR
[The vast wasteland of human potential]

If human progress were only instigated by the wealthy elitist class, then civilization would still be hidden in caves. Most of the new ideas and discoveries in the world have come from people with dreams and a profound desire to escape the miseries of being born poor. The rich enjoy their leisurely lifestyles, while the poor look for ways to improve their economic condition. Being wealthy has little to do with superior intelligence or humanitarianism, or even good business sense. Being wealthy has everything to do with greed, exploiting the labor of workers, and capitalizing on the ideas of others, many of whom are poor people with great ideas, but no avenue to the market.

Being economically disadvantaged, however, does not eliminate hope and dreams. Since necessity is the mother of invention, imagine how many inventive minds are working overtime among the vast wasteland of human potential that is poor. The poor receive little respect in our society. They are seen as burdensome, looking for handouts. One out of five persons in America are among the working poor. They toil at several low paying jobs, to raise large families. They are usually so tired, that even their inventiveness remains dormant. As a result, the seeds of progress that are contained in the minds of the poor do not receive the water necessary for germination. And the great minds that could have been, never become available to benefit the continued evolution of civilization.

77 - POPULATION CONTROL
[The boat is swamped, and going down on its own weight]

What economic, ethical, political, or spiritual justification exist for the prolongation of the human lifespan in a world that is struggling with overpopulation and environmental pollution, depletion of the top soil, deforestation, global warming, nuclear and chemical pollution, and destruction of the ozone layer. These outcomes continue to be exacerbated by the world's population explosion.

What incentive is there for saving lives when the earth's human population growth is threatening the very existence of all life? By the year 2050, in 54 short years, at the present rate of growth, the earth will need to support 50 billion people, which is almost ten times the world's present day population of 5.5 billion people. Where will the food come from to feed so many mouths, when the top soil is disappearing at 2 to 5 percent per year? Where will we obtain sufficient supplies of fresh drinking water, when humans waste 95 percent of their water supplies, while polluting potable sources? Where will people store all of the trash and toxic wastes, much of which takes a millennium to decay?

Perhaps killer diseases are the natural method of controlling overpopulation and its negative consequences on the biosphere. Another is starvation. Starvation heightens disease in the third world, as weakened bodies are more susceptible to

126

Infections and diseases. If the poor, aged, disabled, handicapped, and non-productive members of the species are allowed to suffer and die, there would be more room for those productive people and that of the elitist classes to prosper. While this idea appears to be inhumane, natural selection is survival of the fittest. In human societies, survival of the fittest are those who command wealth, knowledge, and power.

With the promising advances in eugenics, there is a possibility of the eradication of the effects of disease while enhancing longevity and sustained youthfulness. Will these miracles of science be for the common people? Or will life extension be gifted only to the wealthy elite? If all the people of the earth were allowed to continue at an unchecked pace of procreation, then eugenics will be a curse, keeping people alive to fight for air, food, water, and space, while the world teeters on mass famines, and eventual extinction. It is only through responsible programs of forced population control, that we can ensure there will be a world left for our grandchildren, and that massive disease, starvation, and inhumane conditions will not be our legacy to the future generations of human beings.

The earth holds limited resources to sustain life. There is a maximum number of people that can be sustained by the biosphere. Governments should agree on ways to prevent humans from the overpopulation that can only lead to destruction and extinction. Forced sterilization at the fetal level may be a necessary step in the future to guarantee that the human population will remain in check. The social and moralistic issues must be confronted and worked out by government soon. Apathy will become the death dirge for us all.

78 - POVERTY

[Institutionalized inhumanity]

Poverty is not a natural condition of human survival. Poverty was non existent among native American tribes, until after they were ravaged by diseases brought by white settlers, their numbers annihilated by white soldiers, their food supply slaughtered almost into extinction, and their land taken by force and broken promises. African tribes did not know poverty until after Europeans kidnapped and broke up their families for the lucrative slave trade, and subjected their peoples to colonial rule. Latin tribes did not know poverty until white explorers ransacked their lands in search of gold, then converted their so-called pagan ways into Christianity. Asians cultures once flourished while the white Europeans nation states fought each other and live as barbarians. Poverty was a white European phenomenon. But after European military conquest and colonial rule, Asia's people suffered great poverty.

The commonality in poverty is that it was a white European export. The white man saw cultures that were rich in natural resources, food, and were in balance with nature, without pollution; then they destroyed these civilizations one by one. They took the wealth of these peaceful cultures, and gave them poverty in exchange. Now, through the greed that was a primary driving force in Europe, the entire world has been polluted with monetary motivation. The wealthy utilize governmental bureaucracies to create economic circumstances that enable them to magnify their wealth, taking away resources and shouldering working people with the tax burden, while they accumulate more wealth through tax loopholes and shelters designed for the rich. Consequently, poverty becomes institutionalized due to the absence of adequate funds to pay for humanitarian programs that help the poor to uplift themselves. Poverty has been the white European legacy to the world. God help us.

79 - PREJUDICE
[Being afraid of the unfamiliar]

The foundation of prejudice can be traced to early childhood development. Infants test their environments and experience pleasure or pain, as their brains become conditioned to seek gratification, while they fear, and thus, try to avoid potentially painful stimuli or situations. They learn to seek stimuli that gives pleasure to their senses, but in their worlds of trial and error, sometimes they get burned or hurt.

Through painful experiences, they learn to use caution, and begin to fear the unknown and untried. This process continues through childhood into adulthood, and imagined fears surface as prejudice. Adults become uncomfortable in new, unusual, or unfamiliar surroundings. They prefer to be in more predictable, thus safe environments. They seek associates who are similar in interests, experiences, beliefs, and even physical traits. Once group identification becomes part of self-image, slender people ridicule overweight people; men and women develop stereotypes of each other that keep them from honest communication; people are not accepted fairly on account of their skin color, clothing style, hair style, poverty, educational level, career, speech accent, or whatever.

Prejudice reflects peoples' inability to deal with reality due to fear. By avoiding or rejecting differences from the tried and true comfort zone, they attempt to create a reality bubble that bounces away from unfamiliar and potentially unpleasant people or situations. Confident people with a healthy self-image, who are in touch with reality do not rely on prejudice for self-protection. Positive people embrace life and all of its joys, surprises, and occasional unpleasantness. They don't want to limit the scope of their experiences and learning by prejudice. Open-minded, accepting people who respect themselves and others seek to engage in dialog, interaction, and sharing. Would it be reasonable for a space explorer to want only to explore the moon, because it is close and familiar; but not want to venture to Saturn because the rings look unusual and foreboding? Let this world be filled with space explorers who seek to experience all that life has to offer, then prejudice dies.

80 - PROGRESS
[Getting out of the rut of stagnation]

Imagine your life without automobiles, electricity, or hot water, and you've imagined your life without progress. Imagine having only one book to read, or one movie to watch, or one television channel, and you're imagining a lifestyle of stagnation. People enjoy socializing and recreation, playing games. But playing games is just that, play. The purpose of progress is to elevate the human condition, to make life better for people. We develop better ways to store food, more reliable means of transportation, improved methods of communications, and more effective medicines. We improve the living standards of all human beings through progress.

The progress hasn't come free. The price of progress has been the gradual destruction of the planet earth, the extinction of its wild life and plants, the loss of it's natural beauty. The rush to exploit the monetary opportunities created by progress has blinded people to the dreadful consequences of unrestrained progress during the past millennium. In search for better weapon systems, humans now live under the dark cloud of nuclear terrorism or cataclysmic war. In search for biological and chemical weapons of war, nations have stockpiles enough toxic substances to kill all animal and human life on this planet at least 1,000 times. In the quest for faster vehicles, thousands die needlessly on our highways, and faster computers are hypnotizing our young, making them into mindless robots who no longer feel comfortable or capable to socialize and interact with others in the real world.

How can we enjoy the benefits of progress without the abysmal side effects and potential destructive outcomes? Environmental scientists search for solutions from nature itself. Microbes that break down toxic wastes into usable organic compounds; harnessing wind, water, and sunlight for energy; recycling glass, metals, paper, plastics, and old tires into building or paving material, and technologies still on the drawing boards that are "clean" can be advanced rapidly if world governments have the long-term vision and commitment. But, sadly, it's easier and less costly in the short-run to pollute and waste, compounding the problems for future generations.

81 - PURPOSE
[Oh why...why...why?]

If we are to accept the premise that human beings are intelligent and are set apart from other animals primarily due to our ability to learn and apply knowledge, then surviving day to day, without a sense of purpose, attainment, and self-fulfillment is simply wasteful. To live without asking, just to die without answers is existing, and not living. If who we are at the present is the sum total of who we have been in the past, then shouldn't we take an inventory of who we have become, and what significant experiences and insights led to the development and acceptance of what and where we are?

Those who are happy living lives similar to that of dogs, going from mate to mate, smelling hydrants, and marking its territory, would not be interested in taking an inventory of anything. Dogs leave their droppings, then move on. Many people are like dogs. They are happy if they get attention and rewards, perform a few tricks for their masters, play, eat, do bodily functions, and sleep; just to do it over again the next day, with no sense of goals or plans, or what's really happening in the world outside of their own block. In some respects, ignorance is bliss; but a person who has self-awareness can not accept a life as dogs. As the ultimate of God's creation on this earth, we are obliged to answer to a higher calling, to utilized our superior minds for positive contributions.

As our lives unfold through our experiences and knowledge, it is often near impossible to get a handle of who and where we are due to constant pressure, stress, and competing priorities from our loved ones, family, friends, employers, government, and the unexpected situations that sometimes cause severe disruptions in our routines. Constructively reviewing and analyzing the past may provide the brain with exercises and methods to make accurate snap shots of where a person has been; where they are going; what and who they have become and the things they have accomplished in life.

Once a person has taken an inventory of their life, they will become more focused on appreciating the present, and be better equipped to make better decisions that will impact the type of future that will unfold. To know the past sets a person free to move more positively into the future, and will greatly minimize the commission of past mistakes.

Once a life inventory has been completed and is read over again, it becomes a motion picture of a person's inner most thoughts. It stimulates an increase in the level of contentment and happiness. Ignorance is not bliss, it's just plain ignorance. Knowledge leads to happiness, if it is used to restructure and redirect energy and effort to build a more productive and fulfilling lifetime.

82 - RACISM

[Why learn to read if a book can be judged by its cover?]

Racism is absolutely the dumbest form of prejudice that people have ever invented. In the case of normal prejudices, people have learned through experience to avoid certain types of situations that have brought pain, like a child who gets burned by a flame. In the case of racism, people will avoid and hate groups of human beings because their skin coloration is darker, lighter, shaded, or tinted unlike themselves. Most prejudices are outcomes of fear, low self-esteem, and cowardice, as reaction to past negative experiences. Racism is groundless, as people cast judgment on billions of other humans due to stereotyping and imaginations, with little, and usually without any interaction or personal exposure to the victims of discrimination.

While every culture has developed a set of rituals and propensities, including racial biases, relying on racial differences as a basis of judgment and decision-making is a throw back to the dark ages of warring states, imperialism, and colonialistic conquests. Racism is a reminder of how easy it is for human beings to de-evolve. Until such time as people can learn to get along, and not allow race to be the most pervasive and divisive issue in their lives, then humans will not, and can not evolve to a higher level of consciousness and humanity. Civilization can not progress while its people dwell in conflict over superficial differences such as skin color.

83 - REALITY
[Real is what you make it]

Physical reality exist which can be quantified and measured. A gun is discharged, a bullet pierces a person's heart, the person drops the ground, and the last dying breath is taken. That is real. Metaphysical philosophers may state that the person in this instance is not really dead, and that life itself may only be perceptions, and only as real as people's imagination. Then imagine the person who is killed in this example as being the believer in metaphysics.

Too often, people delude themselves by selectively perceiving, and rationalizing the consequences of their actions or inactions, or the outcomes of circumstances beyond their control. They can not accept the negative and unexpected events that impact their lives, thus they look for explanations, excuses, or even straight out lies to escape reality. How often have police heard the excuse, "I was not speeding, but only going with the flow of traffic", and honestly believed it. And how does the Sunday church going Christian explain how they got drunk on Saturday night, then had extramarital sex? Answer, things just sorta happened...it wasn't like it was planned. Anyway, God forgives people for their sins, and it wasn't really bad because it was consensual, and no one got hurt. So they say.

It would be interesting to have people wear mini video cameras for even a day, then to interview them at the end of the day to compare what they remember about their perceptions. Discounting incidents of forgetfulness, the reliable memories would certainly demonstrate perceptual and interpretative distortions of reality. How then can people ever agree on anything in life when the perception of what is real can be totally opposite? How can people begin to discuss solutions to long standing problems when they can't agree on what the problems are in detailed comprehensive terms? Humans have the commonality of five physical senses, but each individual utilizes their sensory apparatus differently to create their personal reality.

84 - RELATIONSHIPS
[Relations move on, as ships sail]

The purpose of building ships is the expectation that they will sail. At least, a boat should float. Relationships do both. For a while, people demonstrate a high degree of caring to the point they seem to be floating. Then, with the passage of time, most relationships set sail, and people move on in their lives. Perhaps it is unnatural to expect permanence in relationships. Neither cultural expectations nor familial blood ties necessarily guarantee either amicability or longevity in relationships. There is no magic bullet to keep love strong enough to overcome the many conflicts large and small that effectively tears a relationship from its mooring. Oftentimes, when people find themselves emotionally trapped in relationships, they pack up their bags and set sail.

While the natural order of both animals and human beings appears to be one of affiliation, the pressures of increasingly complex social interaction, changing and confusing situational ethics, abrogation of individual responsibilities, and legislated or institutionalized intrusion into defining appropriate role behavior has brought about a high level of apathy and alienation that pervades people's daily lives and affairs. Relationships bend to the stress and strains of society's onslaught of what is politically correct, as people try to conform to the superficialities of public appearances. Individualism and even common sense is replaced by jingoes, contrite aphorisms, and pretense that fails to effectively substitute for communication and honest interaction. People look at each other, talk to each other, and spend time together; but eventually find that the person who had occupied the status of partner was only occupying proximal space; as the person with whom they were enraptured was never truly present.

85 - RELIGION
[The opiate of the common people]

What would the world be like without organized religion? Certainly, there would be a lot less ornate, statuesque, and towering buildings. Perhaps the world would be more chaotic, violent, and dangerous. Or maybe people would adjust to the lack of religious guidance, and have less reasons to bicker about differences in faith and beliefs. Perhaps millions of people would not have been burned at the stake, burned in death camp ovens, beheaded, and otherwise killed in the name of various righteous gods, or in defiance of religious orders.

It is interesting that religion appears to affect common people more that those who own the financial resources of society. In most cases, preachers, ministers, pastors, mullahs, and even apparently ascetic monks live better than the average working poor or peasant. Besides the original spiritual leaders, such as Christ, Mohammed, Buddha, and devout practitioners such as Ghandi, Malcom X, and Dr. Martin Luther King, almost all leaders of the world's organized religious sects live lives of splendor. Only the wealthy rulers and financial barons experience lives of comfort that exceeds those of highly respected spiritual leaders. Their positions of enlightenment gives them a special charisma to garner great influence with the ruling class, as the common fodder gladly part with their hard earned minuscule belongings to bolster the elevated lifestyles of their religious leaders and rulers.

Are average people so insecure and confused about their own beliefs and behavior that they must flock to religious leaders to hear how evil people have been, and how they deserve spiritual death unless they conform to a set of spiritual rules, among which conveniently is the rule of giving financial support to the religious leaders? Religious absolution of peoples' guilt is not free, as it addicts millions of true believers and week-end spiritualists to endorphin "fixes" that are naturally released in their brains when in certain emotionally heightened states of religiosity.

[Time travel to distorted memories of better times]

"Here's one for the Gipper." A phrase often used by then President Ronald Reagan in reference to his movie star days, when his life was more glamorous than burdensome. Even though he was never more than a "B" actor, his distorted memories of a glamorous past gave him a sense of immortality, an escape from the constant pressures and responsibilities of being the most powerful man on earth. It is common for people to reminisce, to daydream about enjoyable moments or happy times in their past. Pleasant memories can offer people a secure vicarious experience. Unfortunately, the human brain does not accurately recall the past, especially as the period of time increases between the event and the recollection.

Personal reality is a subjective phenomenon that may or may not be verifiable by others. Once people have fulfilled their hierarchy of physical needs, then emotional, mental, and spiritual needs are drives that interact to color perceptual reality. Memory and desire often conspire to produce a subjective reality that fulfills certain non-physical needs. People who "live in the past" literally dwell in retrospective thoughts, memories, and fantasies. Retro-music, retro-style clothing, classic cars, Victorian homes, and classical movies provide retrogressive stimuli that enhances the recapture of the "feel" of past realities.

While retrogression in itself can be enjoyable and fulfills various people's emotional needs, it can become an obstacle to an honest assessment of the present reality, thus inadvertently preventing responsible decision making that is rudimentary to affect future outcomes. People who still relish in the fantasies of a better time when black people were slaves bias their perception and acceptance of the present reality. This type of retrogression transforms into negative thoughts and actions that hinders the progress of society and civilization, and more importantly, the ethical evolution of the human species.

87 - RICH
[Does that make them better than the rest?]

The most common wish among average people is their desire to be rich. The proliferation of government sponsored lotteries attest to the value and high regards that people place on monetary wealth. People are admired for the property that they own. Luxury cars and mansions. Fine clothing and cuisine. Purchasing power. The owners of material things gain respect, that as people they may not deserve. People become rich primarily through one of three methods. One-third of the rich people inherit their wealth. One-third earn it. One-third obtain it through exploiting loop-holes in the law or by deceiving many others into losing their hard earned money. All three groups typically own estates, investment properties, stocks, and luxury automobiles. Without knowing the background of wealthy individuals, a drug lord, corporate executive, or shrewd investor all receive a formidable level of public respect. It is only once a person's private dealings are exposed that public perceptions change. Drug lords shy from publicity due to the nature of their enterprises. Benefactors start charities that usually bear their names. People who have done it the hard way, usually shun humanitarian pursuits, feeling that if they could make it, then less capable or lazy people don't deserve wealth.

Stripped of their positions of wealth, the material comforts, political influence, and respect received would evaporate. Commoners when naked before our Creator, all with similar human physical traits when first born, and dying as aged imperfect bodies when the time comes. Perhaps people would do better to look beyond the external packaging, to reveal the heart of the person before ascribing laurels bases on wealth alone.

88 - RIGHTNESS
[Justifying and defending moral convictions]

During the most recent period of European imperialism and colonialism, "white made right" because "might made right". Since the beginning of the race toward world conquest, various European nations have had their blood soaked periods of inhumanity to others, both non-white as well as whites. Five hundred years of white domination of non-white peoples on planet earth finally ended with the overthrow of apartheid in South Africa. Now right no longer is a function of the race of the conqueror, but rather a more universal recognition and respect for all people on earth.

Religious differences still divide the world's people into various sects and camps. But examination of the basic tenets of the major organized religions of the world discloses basic agreement in certain universal principles of love, self-sacrifice, honesty, worship, and recognizing the evils of greed. Yet various religious groups battle over who is absolutely right. Its members are inspired at times toward martyrdom, mass homicide, and other acts of inhumanity. Acts that seem to overshadow the concept of rightness by the extreme wrongness of the outcomes.

Rightness appears more to be a justification or rationalization for negative actions taken by individuals, groups, or governments. In order to be absolved of guilt for wrongful acts, people conveniently discover religious passages and statements, then apply them often out of context to explain their acts, thereby escaping the personal responsibility for any negative intentions and outcomes of their actions. Until the peoples of the world move closer to a universal concept of humanity, rightness as defined by competing religious orders will continue to divide rather than to unite.

89 - ROLE MODELS
[Imprinting the positive]

Michael Jordon, Mohammed Ali, Wilma Rudolf, Jackie Robinson, Jerry West, Carl Lewis, Tommy Lasorda, John F. Kennedy, Robert Kennedy, Abraham Lincoln, Franklin Delanor Roosevelt, General Douglas McArthur, General Colin Powell, and Dr. Martin Luther King. Athletes, sportsmen, Presidents, and military men. Heroes to many, martyrs for humanitarian causes, and fighters for freedom and justice. All role models who set standards of conscience, self-sacrifice, and honest hard work for the rest of society to emulate. Great men who rose to the challenges of their times, whose speech and actions boosted humanity during some of its darkest hours, or whose inspiration elevated the spirits of all people during the course of their lives.

After ducklings are hatched, they follow the mother duck around to emulate her actions, learn to swim, and develop social relations with their siblings. Scientific research has demonstrated that in the absence of the mother duck, the ducklings will follow whatever takes the role of mother, imprinting on the scientists who conducted the studies. People also possess imprinting instincts similar to that which are found in most animal species. Learning appropriate behavior is essential to the survival of the young of any species, when they are most vulnerable to the hostilities that exist around them. If the young are taught by destructive examples, they'll display destructive behavior. If positive role models are presented to children early in their development, they'll probably imprint on constructive actions that will set their standard of behavior for the rest of their lives.

Crime and violence has become more prevalent in American cities due to the break down of the nuclear family; negative role models which are depicted in music, television, and the movies; and persistent poverty that institutionalizes alcohol and drug addiction. Where do children find positive role models anymore? All around, heroes are fallen. Americans once looked to politicians to inspire them to greater heights, but many politicians have themselves fallen to the greatest depths. Watergate, Iran-Contra, Nicaragua, and have been scandals that struck down the public trust and confidence in its leaders. Policemen are convicted of drug dealing, rape and murder. Firemen are convicted of multiple arson fires. Athletes are rejected for drug use and illegal gambling. Religious leaders are defrocked by the weaknesses of their own flesh. Parents are found guilty of abusing, molesting, raping, and murdering their own children. Wives and husbands fight to the bitter end, often resulting in homicide.

It is no wonder society is witnessing an unprecedented increase in the level of crimes and violence being committed by its young. Kids as young as 6 years old beat one year old children to death. Twelve year old boys rape nine year old girls, and murder 89 year old grandmothers. These outcomes can be directly correlated to the prevalence of negative role models, and the relative absence of positive role models in the lives of people, especially children. Ducklings imprint, and apparently, people are more like ducks than human beings. It's long overdue for society to emphasize positive Olympian achievements again to elevate the human spirit of its future generations.

90 - ROMANCE
[Making a play of it]

Everybody needs love. Love makes the world go 'round. Cliches; but were this not to be overwhelming more true than not, these types of sayings would cease to exist. Ask a thousand people anywhere in the world if they would agree with the universal need for love, and why they think this is a truism. Their probable explanations would fall into one of the following categories:

1. The creator made us this way.
2. Love is good, and hate is bad. Love conquers evil.
3. In an evolutionary sense, if there was no need for love, humans would have long become extinct. It's a basic survival instinct that continues the species.
4. Without the need for love, there would be no romance.

All of the above explanations are true at times, depending on the individual. Most people at one time or another have spent much effort, time, and money in pursuit of romance, to find the process of attracting a love interest to be a challenge with unpredictable outcomes. People have rationalized unsuccessful attempts to obtain the objects of their affection by creating a series of explanations, excuses, and theories, including some of the following:

1. It's random chance, the luck of the draw.
2. It's mostly physical attraction, the eyes have it.
3. It's the way a person dresses to impress.
4. It's mostly personality, charm, and wit.
5. A person is more attractive when they're already married because they become a challenge; and married persons are emotionally safer because they usually won't risk their marriage.
6. A person is less likely to attract another when they are in need because they may appear desperate, so there must be something wrong. People need more of a challenge.

7. People seek confidence in others because it makes them feel more secure as part of their socialized need.
8. Some people give off more pheromones.
9. When it rain, it pours; you get more when you don't need or want it (like credit).
10. The bigger the better (not in reference to brains).

Professed nightclub gadflies have summed up a method for attracting people.... good looks; then it's a matter of bucks, drugs, alcohol, or luck to get the f.... We could go on, but suffice it to say that all of the above are probably true to some extent all the time, to varying degrees, depending upon the object of one's attraction.

Accepting physical limitations, people turn to emphasizing other attributes in an effort to attract the people they desire. Seeking love and romance, and not just sexual gratification, is conducive to the process of courting. The romantic dinners, sunset walks along the beach, watching the city lights or stars from the foothills and mountains, long drives where couples could talk and get to know each other, making love in front of a fire place during a winter evening or on top of a hill during the spring. Inspirational romantic events.

Most people tend to be more physical in their approach to courting. Ask 1,000 people at what point they began to fall in love, and 90% will probably admit that it involved touch, desire, and some physical intimacy. The process of being naked and vulnerably exposed, then making love provides a natural circumstance for mutual acceptance. Unfortunately, many people fail to see the vulnerability aspects of intimacy, and the trust that it could engender; consequently, they perceive the "act" simply as the function of sexual gratification, often causing emotional hurt, by rejecting the person that's inside. These emotionally damaged people subsequently create emotional blocks and barriers, becoming wary and suspicious of others in general, so when a real good-hearted person comes along, even back flips may not be good enough to earn trust. In return for respect and good treatment, we often find these damage people seeking the same abusive types again, as a way to work out deep-rooted unresolved questions. Oftentimes, nice people do come in last, figuratively and literally.

We often hear the cliche, "it's what's on the inside that really counts." But in real life, the goodness on the inside rarely seems to count for very long when in comes to romance. People seem more interested in what's on the outside, the packaging, the shiny paint job. Money, power, sex, glamor, and fame seem to be more predictive of attracting "love" than internal attributes that are not readily seen or appreciated. Oh, well....

91 - SECURITY
[Another falsehood notion's time has past]

From the first day an infant lays against its mother's bosom, it seeks the feeling of comfort and security. As children, the nuclear and extended family social system had provided a sense of security and connection; but as social interaction in schools, at work, and at the playgrounds alienate people, the trust and feeling of safety and security is replaced by apprehension, uncertainty, and fear. No one is guaranteed a life of dignity. The homeless wander and eat from trash bins. Drug addicts wake in rat infested crack houses surrounded by trash and infective hypodermic needles. Children sell their bodies for another day's survival. Society's forgotten humanity. No one seems to really care. Politicians respond with laws which will make entire families homeless within 2 to 5 years. And the cycle accelerates.

People were once secure in their families, jobs, and neighborhood. They trusted their neighbors, their ministers, public officials, politicians, lawyers, teachers, and doctors. Now people are so often confused that they can't even trust themselves. Security is becoming an unspoken word, an archaic ideal. Public apathy and disillusionment has created massive fatalism and self-centeredness. Corporations deal the death blow to untold millions of households, forever changing the lifestyles of its members forever by downsizing its work force in the search for greater profits for its chief executives and stockholders. If our government is indeed to be a government of the people, for the people, and by the people, then why does it stand by idly while the people's basic desire for security is being abrogated and abandoned?

92 - SELF-IMAGE
[Mirror, mirror on the wall...who's that looking back?]

Most people define their self-image within a broad range accepted as the social norms for beauty and ugliness. Acquisition of attributes such as titles, wealth, power, and fame are attempts to bolster self-image through external sources, often to the neglect of internal character, emotional, and spiritual development. People who are driven by a feeling of inadequacy will often compensate through activities which attract the approval or praise of others. Most entertainers, athletes, politicians, and people in the public limelight have a deep rooted need for acceptance that motivates them to great achievements. Most people have from the time of infancy, sought the approval of others. Acceptance and accolades appear to fulfill a basic emotional need that is inherent to human nature. Perhaps it is a primordial DNA trait that permitted humans to band together socially, thus improving the survival rate of human beings as a species.

Self-image is a cumulative portrait of oneself as reflected back to them by society's social value mirror. Self-image changes in reaction to social stimuli, norms, and judgements. Even hardened individualist or leaders compare themselves to the norm, to reassure themselves that they stand above the crowd. No person is an island totally to itself. Even islands are surrounded by vast oceans, teaming with life that invariably impacts its environment. In the same way, as long as people live among others, they are inadvertently affected, and their self-image is altered through interaction with their social environment. Even the person who does no more than sit before a computer screen is being affected and defined by the engaging activities, and the self-image will incorporate the values imparted thereof. In the great collective that is the cumulative affect of all people in every society, each person develops an individual self-image that reacts to the whole.

93 - SEXISM
Politicians legislating personal attitudes]

What is sexism? Thirty years ago, the word itself didn't exist in that era's latest edition of Websters Collegiate Dictionary. God made Eve from Adam's rib. And almost every society since that time has had men as the dominant gender in almost every activity. Male dominance was and is still manifested in preferential disparity in almost all of life's activities and social roles. Male chauvinism, superiority, and dominance has largely been accepted and institutionalized throughout the entire world. Statistics bear out the preference given to men in economic opportunities, social freedoms, career choices, familial role dominance, and political power. It wasn't until the 1920s that women could vote in America, and it was still a taboo for women to openly express their desire to enjoy sex until after the 1960s.

In most societies, women still take the back seat, and fulfill roles as homemakers, providing maintenance and emotional support of their husbands and children. Even in a technologically advanced society such as Japan, over 90 percent of female college graduates can rise no higher than secretary or retail clerk. Less than 5 percent ever make it at a professional level, in management, or as doctors, lawyers, and politicians. Their role is primarily to support their husband's parents through their years of senility. It is primarily in the west, in societies of Anglo-European stock, that the greatest gains are being made for women's' equal rights. Women are rejecting male dominance, and are utilizing their improved economic and political stature to gain governmental support of their causes.

Unfortunately, some of the laws passes have been designed to pander to statistics that indicate females to be an increasingly formidable voting block. However, poorly written laws, while giving the impression of guaranteed equal rights to women, actually creates a backlash effect that hurt women in the long run. Women now turn their attention from sexual discrimination and harassment at the work place to division on issues such as abortion, pornography, sexual preference, and religious leadership. The backlash against women shows up brazenly as legislation against affirmative action programs, and phasing out welfare benefits.

Opportunities for the exploitation of women's bodies is at an all time high, garnering participants executive level tax-free income for all forms of sexually oriented entertainment. And even in legitimate movie making, the stripper has become a role model. Gains made in one arena are often losses in another arena. Feminists are themselves in conflict; in disagreement over the individual right of women to partake in images and activities that degrade women, as long as it's the exercise of their individual choice. Is a woman who is a college graduate exercising her female rights in her choice to be a high-priced call girl, as long as she either freelances, or works for a madam, versus working for a pimp?

Can anyone define sexism anymore, or has the concept, only after thirty years inclusion in the lexicon of civilization, become an empty and non-distinct part of political satire?

[The journey continues]

Humans actually made it to the moon! Now, humans orbit the earth for extended periods, covering distances equal to four round trips to the moon, approximately 2 million miles, in a little more than a two week period. At this rate, a round trip to Mars could be possible, traveling 100 million miles within a two year period (though the use of booster rockets could shorten the trip to a year). The problem of space travel is not much related to the predictability of technology, but instead is limited by the unpredictability of human physiology and psychology. The affects of extended confinement and weightlessness on humans appear to be debilitating; causing increased skeletal brittleness and middle ear equilibrium problems, while mental and sensory faculties appear to lose functionality with increased time in space. What good would a manned trip to Mars or to Saturn (8.5 years) be worth if the human astronauts would become babbling idiotic quadriplegics by the end of their voyage?

Not withstanding a quantum leap in space travel technology that would drastically reduce travel time, manned space travel as envisioned by present day science is limited to earth's backyard. Travel to Venus, Mars, and Mercury might be possible within another generation, once travel times can be shortened to months versus years. Deep space travel could be possible once nuclear and positronic propulsion systems are developed to propel payloads at extremely high speeds into distant sectors of our universe. Gaining a greater understanding of human's relative place and standing in the universe certainly would provide source material to support, modify, unify, or refute conventional scientific theories and religious dogma. Or perhaps humans would be faced with superior life forms from distant worlds, some of whom may be interested in conquering an inferior terrene population.

The history of animal life on earth, including that of human beings has been one of conquest. The strong has always conquered the weak. This principle appears to be a universal outcome in the natural world. There is little reason to believe that this basic principle is not in effect in other parts of the universe, since all that is came from the same creation of time, matter, energy, and space. As infants in the quest for space travel, we would be the weak prey should we ever be confronted by seasoned space travelers. Predatory species could exploit or destroy human civilization at will. We can not assume that superior intelligence and technology would translate to enlightened peaceful exploration by extraterrestrial beings. Then again, perhaps it would not be illogical to deduce that were there to exist superior extraterrestrials who are capable of deep space travel, that over the 15 billions years life span of our known universe, that the earth is not already at their mercy.

Whether a lion cub ventures out of his cave to explore his environment, or stays in the lair, there is no guarantee that the busy hyenas would not attempt to prey on the innocent, either out in the open, or right in the lion cub's home. The qualitative difference is that the lion cub that explores its environment, learns to overcome and defeat foes, thus becoming better prepared for survival in unforeseen circumstances. Similarly, were humans to stay at home and not reach out to the unknown, we would not have the necessary experience through trial and error to meet a potential foe on equal grounds. The more humans attempt to explore space, the greater he will prepare for unforeseen cosmic eventualities.

95 - SPECIAL INTERESTS
[Backroom deals and steals]

Why do some people seem to have an inside track on promotions at the workplace, while other seemingly more competent people remain locked in the same position well past their time? Why are so many laws passed that benefit only selected groups? Why does government subsidize large corporate farmers not to grow crops, or dairymen not to milk cows? Why are large portions of public lands leased to corporate developers for close to nothing, and oftentimes costing taxpayers a sizable loss of income? Why are corporate executives and certain stockbroker pals able to get the jump on the stock market, and make big killings before large portfolio managers can reacted, or long before John Q. Public reads the stock reports in the business section of the local newspaper; consequently leaving them to suffer losses to pay for insider trading gains? Why is there massive cover-ups of wrong doings at all levels of the economy, in both the public and private sectors? Do backroom deals where the promise of favors, or actual exchange of cash or other gratuities present plausible incentives?

In real life, deal making has always been part and parcel to standard business practice. Laws which prohibit backroom conspiracies serves to give commerce the illusion of free and fair trade; however, the actual practice of commerce is corrupt with special interests and vice at every level, and across the spectrum of business from the liquor store to the corporate boardroom, from the golf course to the motel room, and from the legislative offices to the complementary buffet at a luxurious resort. Most of the inside dealings are invisible as the transactions involve cash or other gratuities (cars, trips, sex, alcohol, drugs, or promise of future benefits, etc.). Whenever large sums of money or the potential for great financial gains is present, the probability of corruption exists.

96 - SPIRITUAL
[Finding peace of mind, if you don't mind]

We have all experienced moments of loneliness, depression, and perhaps even desperation. During those soul searching times, our friends, families, possessions, and activities did little to calm our spirits, or to fill the void in our hearts. Circumstances hit us unexpectedly, and left us severely wounded. We suffered the loss of a loved one through death. We became broken-hearted when our significant other was no longer there for us. We no longer felt loved or appreciated. We lost our job, became bankrupt, and lost our home to the creditors. We suffered a life changing injury. We wished we could change the past, but we couldn't make things right again. Our hearts bled out our souls. We felt that maybe death was a possible solution to the deep emotional pain and void that we felt. We no longer had a reason to live.

But a small voice spoke to us, in our innermost thoughts. It was a voice that said, "have faith, as your time has not yet come."

And like every storm, some lasting longer than others, eventually the sun does shine again. Getting through the emotional storms often requires us to call on our religious beliefs. Faith in God. Some positive force that provides continuity, hope, justice, and love. As children, we first sought those unconditional qualities from our parents, but adult role models eventually disappointed the high expectations of the innocent. As adults, we look to our Father in heaven, God, Jehovah, Allah, Yaweh, or whatever we have named our spiritual creator. We seek a reason and purpose for our suffering. We want a tangible reason to keep on living. Show us a sign that our suffering will soon end. Give us hope for a better day and a better life. Let us know that we are deserving of more.

The power of belief, faith, and prayer has been well documented in mankind's existence. The course of human endeavors and history has often hung in the balance on faith, of serving a higher power than ourselves, and in garnering the courage that comes from belief in the righteousness of our purpose and the support of our God. Even the most powerful rulers of our times have fallen to events that they could not stop. Common people who had the belief in a higher spiritual force have toppled governments, and continue to exert great influence on the socio-economic and political fiber of almost every society in the world.

Unfortunately, the socio-economic influence of various organized religions has fostered a climate of divisiveness, occasionally resulting in horrendous atrocities against people during the course of history and into the present time. So called holy men turned organizations into mechanisms of power, prestige, wealth, and influence; often becoming the objects of reverence and worship themselves. Many claims of healing the sick and raising the dead by touch or prayer could be witnessed by those wanting to believe. Magicians, whose clever illusions would have resulted in witch hunts only 300 years ago, now enjoy great fame and fortune, as do modern day televangelists. Many people have become estranged from organized religion, and prefer to pray directly to God.

97 - STREET SMART
[Reading people's fears, desires, and motivations]

Street smart people are adept at "con jobs" that they do on honest and naive people due to clever deceptive ploys that are not usually found in books. The dynamics required for survival on the streets utilizes similar principles of interaction and deception that are used in the corporate boardrooms, only the faces and situations differ. Street smart people are also expert negotiators and observers. They can size up a person's motivation, desire, and weaknesses by noticing body language, listening for vocal inflections and choice of words, and facial expressions that present a subliminal language that can be accurately interpreted by the astute street wise person. The experienced street hustler is like the fox let loose in the chicken pen, knowing exactly the strategy needed to steal the chicken eggs, or to kill the chickens.

It is sometimes said that those who are unable to earn a decent living from their knowledge become teachers. Street hustlers who have little formal education are able to manipulate and take advantage of the most educated people who tend to be less socially adept. The college degree simply states that a person has survived the formidable obstacle course as certified by their certificate. There is no guarantee that the years spent in higher learning actually translates to comparable utility in the real world of negotiation, deception, ulterior motives, tactical misinformation, and intimidation. Colleges and universities are big businesses, whose hidden agenda is to make a profit and/or to keep the status quo in the towers of power and prestige.

Students are the docile consumers. The hard streets, store fronts, and corporate offices are the real places of higher education. Only the tough skinned gladiators survive and prosper in the predatory environment of the real world. The wet behind the ear college graduates become cannon fodder for the corporate trade wars, as hardened street smart business executives and ambitious up and coming butt kissers take home the bacon.

98 - SURVEYS
[Right from the source]

Much of life involves questions. Sometimes answers are obvious, but oftentimes, even simple solutions escape us, are not evident, or require us to change our perspective and perceptions.

We are usually prisoners of our life experiences and limited knowledge. We filter reality through our personal sets of values and beliefs whether they can be proven or not. We stand by our theories and explanations of why things are as they are, and soon begin to see our untested conclusions as scientific facts. We pre-judge others based on personal biases and prejudices often founded upon false stereotypes created and fostered by others due to fear or hatred. We fail to show compassion and understanding because we wish to bury our head in the sand. But all those who have buried their heads in the sand exposes their frailties. Then the recriminating questions arise, the shock and surprise... why me? Why not them?

In order to answer questions that arise in the real world, it becomes necessary to research those realities. Many Americans never thought that they would find themselves unemployed, or that they could ever lose their homes, or find themselves in jail for alcohol or drug abuse, or suffer a debilitating injury or illness that forever changes their lives. As with violent crime, these are the realities that suddenly and with little or no warning strike down the minds and hearts of untold millions of Americans each year. And forever they are changed. If we see warfare as man's ultimate inhumanity, then we need look no farther than our own cities to see warfare on our streets. Warfare that inflicts severe lifelong emotional, mental, and physical injuries to our innocent children. Socio-economic warfare that takes away people's hope for a better life. A decay that strikes at the very moral and spiritual basis of civilized societies. Yet, right under our noses, often only a few miles away, the blight is glaring. The plight is pervasive. So we turn our heads, avoid the affected areas, and bury our heads in the sand.

The vast majority of Americans are only one or two paychecks away from joblessness, homelessness, and hopelessness. As the safety net unravels through political insensitivity, more Americans will find themselves in lives of destitute, desperation, deprivation, and degeneration. That is not considered living. Dogs are better kept than that. And the wealthy equity holders of our world's vast resources know that they would rather feed their pets than a starving child on the streets. Where do the answers lie?

Usually the pleads from those most affected the are usually ignored because few bother to ask what they feel could be viable solutions. Policymakers, who rarely experience the socio-economic problems of our times, are more interested in making decisions that enhances their political careers than in finding real effective solutions. They bury their heads in the sand because after 15 years of public service, Congressmen are vested in multi-million dollar pensions that are paid for by hard working taxpayers who are becoming poorer. Take a few hours from your life, and take a public survey on any question that concerns or perplexes you. The experience of the diversity of responses will be an insightful event.

99 - TECHNOLOGY
[A panacea or a plague?]

The march of technological progress can not be stopped, slowed down, avoided, or ignored. Technology has been both a blessing and a curse to humanity. While cures and treatments for diseases has greatly increased the average lifespan; and advances in computer science, satellite communications, and robotics has revolutionized the way people interact with each other in the global village, people should not look to technology to provide the solutions to the most pressing human problems. Technology is far from being a panacea, and it has elements that under certain circumstances can become a plague, such as a massive nuclear or bio-chemical world war.

What are the most important problems in the world? Malnourishment; starvation; ethnic, racial, and tribal warfare; child abuse, neglect, and endangerment; drug addiction; criminality and violence; decay of the nuclear family; government intrusiveness; and various fears are pervasive and persistent. Can technology solve these human problems? No. Only the will of human societies to correct the inequities and injustices that exist in their midst can provide solutions. Another machine, a faster and more accurate computer, and more controllable consciousness altering drugs will not provide the needed answers. If technology continues unchecked, the potential for misuse and abuse is unprecedented.

The race toward greater mass consumption of technology has frightening potential consequences. Irreversible environmental pollution; the proliferation of medicine resistant incurable diseases; nuclear and biological or chemical terrorism; social alienation that leads to mental disorders and sociopath behavior; and massive underemployment may become the future outcomes of technological progress.

100 - THEORIES
[Toward developing a universal perspective]

Since the time we were children, we learned about our environment through trial and error, and thus about ourselves and our limits. In time, we developed various explanations to better understand the apparent randomness of reality in our attempt to categorize our experiences into more predictable and less frightening emotional stimuli. We adopted and associated a series of notions into a belief system that provided a behavioral map to guide us into the unknown, our futures. Occasionally, we found it beneficial or necessary to reinterpret the facts, to change perspectives, or to fine tune our perceptions of reality.

We learned from trial and error, and that which we could not even begin to understand, we explained with folklore, pseudo-science, religion, superstition, or our personal psychic brand of theories on reality. Some became very comfortable with adopting beliefs of various sects, dogmas, rules of belief and conduct that focused the thinking and decision-making responsibility on enlightened leaders; thereby releasing one from personal blame for erroneous actions. We all sought the same basic concept...the truth and the knowledge of what is right and wrong.

Modern science, with its intellectual supporters, has proclaimed itself to be the truth. But upon closer examination, we find many scientific fields to be built upon so called principles and theories which are eventually overthrown and replaced with other explanations that made the old regime obsolete. We have experts refuting experts. Even with our grand technologies, science can not explain many natural phenomena, and we are impotent to affect even one percent of the natural processes such as weather, space, and creation of living things. Human beings are infants when it comes to discovering and understanding the truth of the universe.

Most average people have come into a series of beliefs, many of which are unrelated and in principle may be contradictory, and attempt to stitch a thread of consistency to tie together a coherent philosophy that explains their subjective realities. We mix science, religion, hypothesis, suspicion, dogma, emotional disposition, optimism, physical perception, and fantasy into a complex series of beliefs that purports to explain most of the experiences that we have encountered, and predictably those which we have yet to face... the unknown, our future, and our fate.

We are comfortable in taking for granted that the sun will rise in most places on our small planet the next day. We assume that we will have food to eat and water to drink, and that we will be able to sleep during the night. Our lives become predictable as we go to work, spend time with our loved ones, consume time with recreational and escapist activities, and perform routine chores. Then a great natural disaster occurs. Our lives are disrupted. We are forced to accept the reality, and not our interpretations. We stand as children before the great forces that humbles.

101 - THREE-STRIKES LAW
[Classic example of playing a national pastime]

Let's take a hypothetical scenario that is played out millions of times every year in America. A hardworking, stressed out worker has financial problems that aggravates his marital relationship. He takes to drinking at friends and at the local bars, for happy hour, before he faces his dissatisfied wife and three hyperactive children. His idealized home life now more resembles a three ring circus than a happy cohesive family group.

One day, on his drive home, he exceeds the speed limit and is stopped by law enforcement, who smells the odor of beer on his breath. After a sobriety test, he is hauled down, booked, and jailed. As this was his third drunk driving arrest, he is charged with a first time felony. He receives 6 months in jail, and 3 years summary probation. After serving 3 months, he is out due to prison overcrowding. He is jobless. His wife and children have moved in with his mother-in-law, who hates him, and is glad that he got what he deserved. His wife has filed divorce papers and demands child support payments and alimony. He is depressed, so he returns to drinking.

His license is suspended for one year, so he does not have a legal way to drive, first to look for work, then as a way to go to work. The buses are very inconvenient in his area, and were he to miss one connection, he would lose most any job that he could find. But he gets lucky, and a friend puts in a good word. He starts in a few weeks. Meanwhile, he is trying to put his marriage back together, but his wife will hear nothing of it, and refuses to let him see his children, who despite some crazy noisy times, he still loves dearly. He drives to a friend's house for advice, and some consolation. He drinks to treat his depression, and to escape his reality. Then, while driving on the way home, he is pulled over for failure to make a complete stop at a stop sign (though he was almost stopped). Again the beer breath gives him away, even though he had changed to light beer, and he is jailed for another DUI offense, a second felony, with increased sentencing due to driving with a suspended license. This time he serves 6 months of a one year sentence.

Out again, his life is in ruins. He has no job, no money, no family or friends to turn to, and no more hope. He doesn't care anymore. He has given up. Soon, his hunger turns to anger, and he feels that society spit him out, when all he needed was a better paying job, and some help. He contemplates ways to get out of his predicament, but there are no answers. He has no home, except his old car. He is hungry. He begs for some spare change. A few people help him out. He spends it on alcohol to keep him warm, and to dull his senses and memories. After a while, his hunger annoys him, and he decides to go back to the store, to steal a sandwich.

Unfortunately, he is caught by the clerk. As he already had two prior felonious convictions, this petty theft which would normally be a misdemeanor, was bumped up in severity to a felony, as he was now a repeat offender, a career criminal. The judge laid down the law. Three strikes and he's out. Sentenced to 25 years to life imprisonment. Later, he receives a letter while in jail, that the district attorney is planning to prosecute him for failure to pay child support. And the IRS seized his car, because he failed to file his income taxes several years ago. He needed the cash to pay for the maintenance of his car.

102 - TRUTH
[It will set you free]

There are people walking this earth who have created an intricate web of lies, distortions, exaggerations, concoctions, and untruths for the purpose of self-deception and misleading others. Reality becomes a blur as they must cover up their dishonesty with more lies and fantasies. They become prisoners to their own story tales, attempting to justify actions, behavior, and scenarios of their creation. The house of cards eventually crumbles under its own weight, or someone discovers a major crack in the story line, and pulls out the tentative support beams. At many points in the life of liars, they are faced with the consequences of their deception, and become the main casualty, the outcome of lies. People avoid their association. Family and friends become wary of the falsehoods and pretentiousness. They are left alone, to look for more unsuspecting prey, who too will eventually escape their grasps.

Life would be so much simpler, were people to deal in the truth. Being truthful may not impress people in terms of social status, but in the long run, being truthful will attract similar honest people. Trusting people seek others whom they can trust. Even liars will avoid liars. Being an honest person allows others to see clearly who the person is, to believe what the person says, and to rely on that person's good intentions. People are comfortable with truthful and honest people. A person's life often depends on the truth. A spouse who has unprotected sex outside of the marital bond potentially kills the innocent partner and takes away an important part of their children's future. It would only be fair to confess, to state the truth, so at the least, the one who was not guilty would be able to make realistic decisions. The truth often hurts, but it could save lives, and certainly it can set you free.

103 - UGLINESS
[Imprisoned by superficialities]

When external beauty deteriorates with age or changing social norms, a feeling of ugliness ensues if inner beauty has not been developed. How important is superficial appearances to most people? Cosmetics, hair treatments, skin rejuvenations, diets, vitamins, and exercise programs are popularly consumed by the insecure masses of people, all of whom want to avoid the stigma of being labeled, "ugly." People are afraid to grow old, not because of the debilitation, but because their faces and bodies tend to shrivel up like prunes. They become externally ugly.

Beneath the weather-beaten aged physical bodies often resides a lifetime of experiences, of trials and tribulations, of memories of travel and romances, of great insights and wisdom, of deeply felt emotions, and once finely tuned talents. Were we to look beyond superficialities, we would see character that was forged in the molten magma of survival. We would see profound beauty beyond the appreciation of the novices, and were we to look past the sagging eyelids, drooping mouths, and slurred speech, we would see ourselves, as we shall be someday. So if people shun the aged or the unusual as being ugly, they should look in a mirror, to see themselves as they will be.

104 - VICES
[If it feels good, it's probably bad for your health]

What is it about the human brain and body that causes it to seek the pleasures of self-destructive behavior? Why are humans susceptible to the additive effects of alcohol, drugs, sex, and violence? Were humans to have been addicts early in human evolution, could they have survived the harshness and hostilities of nature? Many civilizations that have developed voracious appetites for vices met similar outcomes; decay and eventual destruction. Why do things that satisfy primal sensory needs act in ways which are so destructive to the physical and mental health of its victims?

Why doesn't alcohol, drugs, and sex act on human beings in positive ways, resulting in increased physical, emotional, and mental health? Why are its results toxic when overused? Is the human being so fragile that it can not naturally adapt to various chemicals and diseases? A list of things that are not harmful to humans is relatively small when compared to the thousands of things that are toxic to human life. The air we breath, the water we drink, the sun that warms us, the food that we eat, the bacteria and viruses that surround us, all cause toxic effects on the body over time. The human body is in a constant state of dying, purification, and cellular rejuvenation. When the balance is lost due to the effects of the environment, the body degenerates more rapidly than it can purify and regenerate, leading to organic dysfunction and eventual failure and death.

Almost everything in life has some toxic effect on the body. It's a matter of degree. Too much of anything tends to overload the body's ability to process the material at a rate that it can handle. Put too much air into a balloon, and eventually it pops. Alcohol abuse leads to liver and kidney failure; drug abuse leads to respiratory and heart failure; sexual promiscuity leads to AIDS and other STDs; and too much food results in obesity, and the predictable heart attack. The social and emotional toll is equally high, with violence, mental illness, and incarceration as probable outcomes. A paradox exists in life; that good outcomes usually require the investment of time and effort, while bad outcomes initially come disguised as effortless and timeless pleasures.

105 - VIOLENCE
[Childish temper tantrums]

Remember back to the first temper tantrum that you had ever experienced and the feelings of violence that you felt. How old were you then? Was this propensity toward anger and violence a learned behavior, or was it a natural experience? How many people do you know that have never felt anger, or displayed its ugly head? A few? More likely, none. Anger and the propensity for violence appears to be inherited, as part of the DNA of each individual. Watch little children, and some will show aggression more often that others, at an age before social influences set in. When little children become angry, they often strike out at others physically as adults laugh and think it's okay and cute because usually no one gets gets hurt. But when this same genetic predisposition is acted out in the real world by adults, people get seriously injured and killed. Societies set in place strict punishments for people who as adults can not control their natural urge toward violent behavior.

The tendency toward aggression and violence, especially among the male of the species has plagued humans for eons. Small tribal societies had pecking order hierarchies similar to that of other social animals, based upon physical aggressiveness. As human societies grew, becoming many civilizations, the meting out of violence became an activity reserved to to ruling class who controlled the military. Thus violence was condoned for specific situations, and punished for all others. Rome had their glorious gladiators. Modern societies have boxing, football, and many violent television programs and movies for vicarious violent fantasies.

Civilization has redirected mankind's genetic propensity for violence into violent imaginations. Unfortunately, there are weak minded people whose desire to act violently can be magnified by violent fantasies, as are typically portrayed in the movies. These individuals eventually are seen on the nightly television news reports as more deranged people. So what's new? Society has come to expect the bizarre and violent. People are fascinated with weird behavior. Something is seriously wrong with our society when hundreds of beautiful, intelligent, young women will throw themselves at a chance to have one night with a mass murderer. Or to marry one, knowing well that they could be the next victim. Charlie Manson, Richard Ramirez, and Jeffrey Damhner all have fan clubs that would make the average man cringe in jealousy.

106 - VOTING
[Taking sides on issues with unrealistic answers]

With the advent of advanced personal computers and sophisticated phone systems that process automated responses, true democracy can finally be available instantaneously. The Constitution of the United States of America provides for a one-man-one-vote form of representative government, which is not a true democracy. A system did not exist back in the 1700s to permit a realistic one-man, one-vote system of government. And if one did exist, the founding fathers probably would have been against "mob rule". Leaders always assume that their judgment is enlightened, while the average citizen may only achieve common sense. Consequently, while technology permits true democracy, no politician would really embrace its outcome to decentralize power, while magnifying options.

Imagine a voting system of instantaneous democratic rule, where people may enter their secret pin number into their telephones, and vote on any impending legislative issues of the day. Abortion or Right to Life? Gay rights or animal rights? Abolition of welfare or immigration? Segregation or integration? Capital punishment or lenient parole? Decriminalization of drugs or capital punishment for drug dealing? Legalization of prostitution, or more pre-schools and childcare? White power or black power? Left wing or right wing? The list is endless. Could, and would common misinformed and uninformed apathetic citizens take the time and interest to make intelligent and responsible decisions that are based upon available data, or would emotionally charged issues create a climate of mob rule, without regards for fundamental rights? Could we have anarchy, with inconsistent and contradictory laws that would cause a law enforcement nightmare?

As it is, there are already too many laws on the books that restrict the freedoms of American citizens in all areas of their lives. There are prohibitions against alcohol, drugs, sex, association, affiliation, the type of cars allowed on public roads, public assembly, commerce, what goes into the water, air, and foods. The list of laws, rules, and regulations is voluminous. Fortunately, representative democracy, while imperfect, does grind at a turtle's pace most of the time, thus limiting the rate new laws could be added on top of old ones. But who knows what this new age of instantaneous interactive mass technology will bring. In the future, technological applications in the field of government could bring great human benefits, or cause calamity, chaos and oppression.

[The ultimate non-solution]

Someday, a religious fanatic will wear a portable nuclear device and in an act of martyrdom, explode it, and take out 200,000 innocent lives. Public sentiment would be hot for revenge, up to and including nuclear retaliation of the major cities in the nations that support terrorism. Whether evidence could absolutely be proven would become a mute point. The faceless masses would want their blood thirst satisfied. Strategic nuclear missiles would be sent to Tehran, Baghdad, and Algiers. No more Saddam, Allahtola, and Kadahfi. But will that stop world terrorism? It would intensify the resolve of religious zealots, to create a rush of paranoia and fear around the globe.

At the present time, there appears to be military detente, and economic competition and mutual trade cooperation on a global level. There are no guarantees that this will remain the status quo while Russian tries to resolve serious economic problems, North Korea threatens South Korea, China threatens Taiwan, Syria/Iran/Iraq/Palestine/etc. are still prone to attack Israel, and political instabilities periodically appear all over the world. Are there any guarantees that India will not explode a nuclear bomb over Pakistan? And what if Iraq's military is able to purchase black market nuclear weapons from the Russian ex-KGB Mafia?

The scenarios for the outbreak of catastrophic wars, including several accidental and near nuclear launches caused by both equipment and human failures, routinely occur. Someday, it may be too late to call a missile back, and the outcome may be straight out of the DOOMSDAY MACHINE.

Feeble attempts have been made through treaties between Russia and the U.S. to scale back on the numbers of deliverable nuclear warheads. The stockpile still amounts to 40,000 or so live warheads. ICBMs are now verified at around 2,000. Submarine launch nuclear missals are frozen at about 4,000. Cruise missiles and nuclear bombs deliverable by planes are not clearly controlled, though the number of B-57s, B-1, and B-2 bombers are known to be less than half of the Soviet fleet of around 500. The beginning of a nuclear war will probably not involve the U.S. nor Russia. It will be in a smaller nations, such as Israel with 200 or so nuclear missiles.

Perhaps India, or another small nation trying to gain international respectability through the development or purchase of nuclear weapons capability. Religious and ethnic differences has now replaced economic motivations as the most likely flash point for a nuclear conflagration. While greed has been a historic factor in the quest to conquer and colonize other lands, there has been a predictable method to the madness. In religious and ethnic strife, the outcomes are not easily predictable, but can be equally catastrophic.

108 - WASTES OF RESOURCES
[Disproportionate distribution]

Enough food is thrown into trash bins at drive-thru restaurants and schools in America to feed tens of millions of undernourished people in a dozen impoverished nations around the world. Four out of five people waste food, leaving on the average a fourth of their plates uneaten, for every man, woman, and child in

America. That amount of food left to rot in trash bins is equivalent to 50 million full meals each day! The average poor person in underdeveloped nations, or the poor in developing nations survive on approximately one-fourth of the daily caloric intake as compared to Americans. The 50 million wasted meals would feed 200 million men, women, children, and the elderly in other parts of the world. The waste of food in America is shameful.

Several other valuable resources are wasted on a massive level. Water, the spring of life, poured down the drains in trillions of gallons each day. Less than 5 percent of precious fresh water is used for our drinking and cooking; 15 percent for bathing and cleaning, 30 percent for washing driveways, watering lawns and golf courses, and the rest is used for agricultural irrigation and industrial processes. There is waste for each type of usage. Drinking fountains waste up to 80% of the water flow, wasting 4 gulps for everyone swallowed.

Showering, and continually running the faucet while brushing or shaving waste 95% of the water that would be required to accomplish the tasks. Agricultural irrigation loses 85% of fresh water due to improper channeling, and industry waste 95% of fresh water because it is primarily used to cool equipment, and is not recycled. Reclaimed water would be more useful for irrigation and industrial use, and automatic sensors should be utilized to regulate personal usage for drinking and hygiene.

Massive application of water conservation could easily, and cost-effectively save up to 90% of all fresh water supplies, so when a cycle of drought strikes, underground supplies would be plentiful.

Energy waste is atrocious. Every hour that a 100 watt light bulb is on unnecessarily in a closet waste some form of natural resource that was utilized to produce the electricity. Coal, diesel, natural gas, nuclear fuel are the primary fuels that are converted by power plants into the electricity that powers cities and industry. Unfortunately, burning fuel adds to environmental pollution. More nature-friendly technologies exist that apply the naturally abundant forces of wind, sun, and surf are not utilized sufficiently to make them cost-effective.

The oil companies want to make the most profit possible from their reservoir of black gold. It will be another 50 years before the strangle hold of oil barons loosens sufficiently to permit fair competition from alternative energy sources. One very promising technology is energy from molecular transformation of water and other liquids and gases through chemical reactions. Even animal, human, trash, and other types of wastes can be harnessed into energy production. There are over 50,000 lightning strikes in the U.S. everyday during the stormy seasons. Surely technology could be employed to harness this great free source of electricity.

Many other commodities are wasted that should be conserved or better utilized. Gasoline, paper, plastic, trees, glass, metals, and so on from A to Z are being wasted, creating more environmental pollution of the air, land, and oceans; wastes that could be better used to benefit humanity and civilization.

109 - WEALTH DISTRIBUTION
[$1000 trillion dollars split 7.3 billion times]

If the world's entire wealth of approximately $1000 trillion dollars could be equally divided among the earth's population of 5.5 billion people, every man, woman, and child would have $180,000 each. Now, the 1,000 richest people in the world own approximately $10 trillion, for an average estate of $10,000,000,000 each (ten billion dollars); and the next top 10,000 richest people in the world combined, own about $500 trillion. This translates to the top .0002 percent of the world's people own over half of its wealth. That means one out of every 550,000 people, or two of every million persons is into mega wealth, with each multi-millionaire averaging fifty million dollars ($50,000,000) a piece.

The next tier of the top one tenth of one percent (0.1%) of the world's population own on the average $10,000,000 (ten million dollars), or in numbers, 5,500,000 people own $55,000,000,000,000 (fifty-five trillion). The next tier of the top one percent of the population (0.9%) which amounts to 50,000,000 (fifty million) people average $1 million each; totaling $50 trillion. The next tier of the top 5 percent of the world's population (275 million people) own on the average $500,000 each or $137.5 trillion.

The next 5 percent of the world's people own on the average $250,000 each, or $68.8 trillion. Thus the top 10 percent of the world's people own $820+ trillion dollars, leaving $180 trillion left for the 90% of the world's population (or 5 billion people), which averages $36,000 for every man, woman, and child. So what's so bad about $36,000? This also happens to be the average annual

177

family income in America. But, realistically, the next 20% of the world's population own $150 trillion (1.1 billion people) or $136,000 each; thereby leaving $30 trillion to the remaining 70% (almost 4 billion people), to share in $7,500 for each man, woman, and child. But realistically, the bottom half of the world's population share in barely $1 trillion, which translates to 2,750,000,000 (2.75 billion people) with a average of $363 for every man, woman, and child. Half of the world's families are worth about $1,000, which is usually their total family income each year. There must be a way to spread the wealth around a little more! It's no wonder millions of children are underfed or starve each day. The shame!

110 - WELFARE REFORM
[There are no free rides]

The government's answer to feeding the poor is to limit the lifetime benefits to 5 years, with a 2 year limitation before able-bodied individuals are expected to find jobs to become tax-paying members of society, rather than society's scavengers. The welfare system in America is actually two-tier, both supported by the tax-paying public. The most obvious is welfare for the poor. The poor consist primarily of uneducated single mothers with more than two young children, without marketable job skills. In addition, the elderly poor, out of the employment pool because they are too weak or feeble to meet the demands of a high output world, depend on government handouts to survive on canned dog food diets. Both groups rely on overcrowded public run hospital facilities; and an increasing number of physicians are no longer treating the poor due to the low reimbursement rate paid out by government programs.

What will happen to the millions of poor people after their measly $300-$400 per month welfare checks, food stamps, subsidized housing, and public health plans are cancelled? What will happen to children, who along with their parent and grandparents will be forced to live on the streets from trash bins and cardboard boxes? Disease, crime, prostitution, molestation, rape, and murder will become commonplace among the poor. Entire communities will become cesspools, ripe for raising future violent criminals. Already, the blighted neighborhoods are riddled with destroyed families and lives, even with the welfare system intact. But, woe be society when these hungry, angry, and hopeless people must commit crimes just to feed their children. The jails, already overcrowded will bust at their seams. Mass rioting and chaos in the inner cities will spill over into the adjacent wealthy enclaves, as tall walls, iron gates, and security guards will become useless against food riots and looting that will occur.

Quick fix politically expedient actions that attack the poor will only exacerbate society's problems, perhaps beyond the hope of any short-term recovery. But that's okay, because the politicians will continue the pork barrel mega-billion dollar welfare subsidies for the wealthy corporations. The rich will continue to dine on caviar and lobster dinners while the poor dine at the trash bins behind the fast food restaurants. The rich will continue to enjoy golf courses at taxpayers' expense, while the poor will live in the bushes that abuts freeway off ramps. Something's obviously wrong with this picture.

111 - WHAT'S LEFT?

[Knowledge begets responsibility]

People have become too complacent about their lives. Their search for comforts and materialism has tainted their ability to seek the truth. Everything in the universe is interconnected, least we humans can even fathom that fact. Everything in this world is interconnected. Dam a river to make a lake, and lives downstream die off. Bust the damn, and the torrential flood kills life that remains left downstream. A child who starves on the streets hurts not only that child, but humanity as a whole. That child's future has been imperceptibly altered, until such time that it affects the lives of hundreds of others. That neglected child could become a mass murderer, a religious zealot, who as an act of martyrdom, explodes a nuclear device in the center of a megalopolis.

Everything, all life, all people are interrelated. As the future is an outcome of the present, the present an outcome of the past, the future is an outcome of the past. Failure to recognize and to act properly on the interconnection of people, time, and events will doom mankind to a cataclysmic end. Nevertheless, life will go on in other distant planets in galaxies that human eyes will never again see, and never again dream of visiting. The human species has been a blight on the history of our planet earth, with the exception of a few bright moments. Perhaps it's our destiny to perish after our brief 15 minutes of fame during the eternal course of time in the universe. But when the human species has met its end time, let distant travelers who venture this way notice that humans were a species that understood their place and felt the interconnection with the rest of God's universe. Let the human epitaph be one that reads, "seekers of truth, accepting of our place in the galaxy, and in communion with the interconnection of the universe". Let's not be discovered by future star travelers as an afterthought; "here lies the remnants of humans beings, the experiment that failed".

The primal man (and men who are intoxicated) display the male's testosterone driven emotionality and behavioral tendencies to become the hunter-killer-rapist persona. The primal female (and when they are intoxicated or under the influence of sexually enhancing drugs) is a whore. There are gender-specific differences between most men and women, regardless of their cultures and race. The cultural rules were created by the dominant gender, the males, which explains why 95% of the world's cultures continue to be male chauvinistic and sexist. And while we hear American feminists and lesbians complain about the white male status quo, 80-90% of the world's women support male role dominance, and are usually attracted to men who fit their expectation of maleness. Few females prefer effeminate men.

When it comes to nice people versus predators and jerks, I estimate that in the American culture of the 1990s who live in large cities, 20% of the people are predators, 10% are scavengers, 20% are suckers (people who are naive, too nice, and gullible), and 50% are in the gray areas, displaying combinations of behavior depending upon the situation, and the type of person they are interacting with.

It will always be the strong dominating the weak. Aggression disrupting peace. Natural laws that were set in motion from the beginning of time dictates these principles in the physical world. The quiet calm lake is made rough by the action of strong winds. The killer shark preys on all other fish. The male lion is the fearless predator in the jungle. Only now, with the advent of computers, do females have an opportunity to be more or less equal to men, but even so, 80-90% of males have computer experience at a young age in developed nations, while only 40-50% of females have less than comparable levels of experience (boys will stay on the computer for much longer periods of time, while girls still prefer to talk to their girlfriends and go shopping, etc). It has always been a sexist world, and it probably will always be so well into the future.

Some things we can change, and others we can only accept, and maybe try to change, without expecting great strides. A new idea rarely takes hold upon its first utterance. People must hear the same idea many times before their internal resistance is lessened, and their mind is ripe for new ideas that they have subconsciously or consciously resisted. When changes come to an entire nation or culture, the conditions must be ripe for change.

The only way women are ever going to be equal to men is to refuse to have sex with them as a bargaining chip for political and economic gains. But that will never happen because sex is a stronger drive for women than for men. Sex for men is like taking a satisfying piss. It tends to be a more penile-specific to brain stimulation experience. Sex for women is like a sensual massage, as it is more of a total body experience. When women have orgasm, their feeling is more intense and longer lasting, often lasting more than 10-15 seconds to minutes. A man's orgasm last only 3-10 seconds. Most women can have multiple orgasms, almost immediately. Most men have to wait at least 10-15 minutes to recover before they can become erect again and have orgasm again. The man's role in sex is usually more aggressive as compared to the woman. Physically, the different body types between men and women predisposes this because a woman needs to feel a man inside her to give her a sense of completeness. A man just needs to stick his penis into any warm hole.

American arrogance has served its purpose to give its populace added confidence needed during nation building and expansion. America was once on the top rung in the hierarchy of nations. While still the most powerful military power in the world (the U.S. military budget is more than all other nations in the world – combined), the effectiveness of that power projection has clearly shown its limitations. Too often American arrogance has been replaced by ignorance and uncorrected will lead to future weakness.

The facts are right out there in plain sight, just as the world was once thought to be flat, that no other planets could possible exist in the universe, that the gods or a God created everything and thus Darwin could not possibly be right. As new discoveries lead to new facts and knowledge, often the old perceptions and paradigms are forced to change.

But why wait for new discoveries when the facts have always been in front of our faces? The Earth was always a sphere, other planets exist in vast stretches of space orbiting billions and billions of stars, some similar to our sun. Too often governments act to punish its populace even though they may make claims of freedom and democracy. The sooner people are willing to remove their tinted glasses or blinders, the more likely they would be able to succeed as the solutions to their problems focus on solving factual versus perceived realities that are hidden in plain view without bias and deception.

www.ingramcontent.com/pod-product-compliance
Lightning Source LLC
Chambersburg PA
CBHW060302290526
45789CB00001B/385